W9-AQI-794

making space, clutter free

THE LAST BOOK ON DECLUTTERING YOU'LL EVER NEED

tracy mccubbin

This book is not intended as a substitute for medical advice from a qualified physician. The intent of this book is to provide accurate general information in regard to the subject matter covered. If medical advice or other expert help is needed, the services of an appropriate medical professional should be sought.

The vignettes in this book are both composite and actual stories of individuals and couples. In some cases, names have been changed for purposes of anonymity.

All brand names and product names used in this book are trademarks, registered trademarks, or trade names of their respective holders. Sourcebooks is not associated with any product or vendor in this book.

Published by Sourcebooks
P.O. Box 4410, Naperville, Illinois 60563-4410
(630) 961-3900
sourcebooks.com

Library of Congress Cataloging-in-Publication Data

Names: McCubbin, Tracy, author.
Title: Making space, clutter free : the last book on decluttering you'll ever
   need / Tracy McCubbin.
Description: Naperville, Illinois : Sourcebooks, Inc., [2019] | Includes
   bibliographical references.
Identifiers: LCCN 2019006715 | (hardcover : alk. paper)
Subjects: LCSH: Storage in the home. | House cleaning. | Orderliness.
Classification: LCC TX324 .M384 2019 | DDC 648/.8--dc23
LC record available at https://lccn.loc.gov/2019006715

Printed and bound in the United States of America.
LSC 10 9 8 7 6 5 4 3 2

To my grandmother, MM,
who taught me not to put down, but to put away.
And also that a cup of tea and good laugh will fix just about anything.

contents

PART ONE

finding the real, emotion-based problem

what's under the clutter?
a new approach

"HI, I'M TRACY. IT'S SO GOOD TO MEET YOU."

That is the first thing I would say to you if you open your front door to welcome me in to tour your home. New friends often ask me, "So...you organize closets?" They imagine me with a P-touch in a holster at my hip and colored storage bins filling the trunk of my van. And yes, I can crush a closet—but I do so much more. By sitting down with me like this for the next few hours, you are metaphorically opening your door to me. I do not take that lightly.

Being allowed inside someone's home to see behind the thriving, successful exterior we throw on every morning and take out into the world—into the places we may not be so proud of—is an act of trust. Especially because what I have discovered over the thousands of decluttering jobs I have done is that when clutter has gotten the upper hand, there is inevitably an emotional root. I call them the Emotional Clutter Blocks, and I have identified seven that come up over and over again when a client has decided to take control of their stuff and live the life they want to be living. Clutter Blocks are the unconscious reasons people hold onto stuff that no longer serves them. In this book, I will teach you about all seven, so you can see which one or ones might be the obstacle between you and your goal for an efficient, beautiful home you can live in with ease. From buying for a fantasy life, to holding onto inherited possessions you don't want, to not letting yourself use the good china, we will explore your clutter and let it tell us the story of where you might be blocked. Then we'll heal that Clutter Block for good.

Remember, whatever you have going on, you are not alone. The woman ahead of you in line at Starbucks with the great shoulder bag? She has a dining table covered in unfolded laundry from last season. Your boss? He actually never has people over because he stopped opening his mail a few years ago. What they have in common are Clutter Blocks. I have spoken at dozens of corporate retreats for top national companies, with people who are leaders in their fields, and they tiptoe up to me afterward and whisper, "That's me. It's like you were talking just to me. I have a Clutter Block!"

In fact, I estimate 90 percent of the homes I enter are in some level of crisis, which creates no small amount of shame, exacting an enormous emotional toll. Since you bought this book, I'm going to guess you are feeling some of the same shame and emotional weight of your clutter. I want to liberate you from all that. I want your home to be a place that you enjoy being in, that helps you quickly and efficiently get out into the world, and that you can share with others as often as you feel like. If your home isn't all three things—restful, helpful, and shareable—then on some level, your home is taking energy from you instead of supporting you to live your best life.

That is where the Clutter Blocks come in. We are going to find out what is standing between your home right now and your vision for how you live—and then eradicate it.

The Clutter Crisis

My company, dClutterfly, has had exponential growth every year since I opened over a decade ago. I now have a team of people under me and a six-week wait list, because the same industrial complexes that created our modern obesity epidemic have created a clutter epidemic, only no one is talking about it in those terms, because by avoiding having people over, we can hide our clutter. It is the crisis behind four walls.

If you are Gen X or older, think back to your childhood. Think back to how many toys you had. Think back to holidays, being *given* something. I bet you could probably remember and name most of the presents you received from ages five to ten. You had *a* doll. *A* bear. You may have even saved some of them to pass down to your own children.

Now think of the bedroom of any kid you know, or if you are Gen Y or younger, think back to your own childhood bedroom. It's a sea of plastic, right? Do you remember hand-me-downs? Hand-me-downs used to be a way of life. It was a given that younger siblings would keep passing along clothes and shoes until they fell apart, and if they didn't fall apart, they went to another family. Consumer goods were *expensive.* Then with globalization and the ability of companies in the '90s to start moving their manufacturing to Asia, items suddenly only cost pennies to produce, and the companies passed those savings on to consumers. Big box store chains grew up to push this new, inexpensive merchandise, and the value of possessions plummeted, with three consequences.

First, we forgot how to care and repair. Which do you want to do on a Saturday afternoon: sit down and sew the hole your chihuahua chewed in your throw pillow, or buy a whole new set for $30? Who do you know under forty who even owns a sewing kit anymore? I am as guilty of this as anybody. I work sixty-hour weeks.

When a new set of tea towels is $2.99, am I going to bleach the old ones after making beet salad? No, they're going in the rag bin, and I'm getting a fresh set.

Second, we got addicted to buying. Make no mistake, it's a dopamine hit. Whether you're clicking "Confirm Purchase" on your iPad or you're standing at the register with your credit card, the act of buying is a high. As our world seems increasingly out of control, shopping feels like an act of taking control. That item was the store's, and now it's yours. You now *have* this, and the feeling of having—be it new towels, a garlic press, or a pair of heels—speaks to the part of your brain seeking a sense of security. "The world can't be falling apart! I have a spiralizer!"

Then, with the advent of Amazon Prime and all the online retailers who have had to offer free shipping to compete, there is nothing holding us back from ordering items all day long on our phones. It is so easy to acquire more than we need and to let the dopamine rush of acquiring become addictive. Because unlike drugs or alcohol, there is no stigma around shopping. In fact, we reward each other for it! You can't show up at an adult cocktail party and say, "I did five shots of tequila on my drive over here!" but you can say, "Look at these great shoes I just got on sale," even though you have dozens of identical pairs already, and you will be met with coos of approval.

The third consequence is that people began using stuff to numb their emotions or bolster sagging self-esteem, to hold onto the past, or to pave the way to an imaginary future. Their possessions stopped being tools and became obstacles.

Although U.S. families have only 3.1 percent of the world's children, we buy 40 percent of the world's toys. The average American home contains over three hundred thousand objects, and since the beginning of the 2009 economic recovery, consumer spending on nonessentials has been the fastest-growing consumer category. We cram our cars and homes full, and then, when we run out of room, three out of four families move the car out of the garage and move more stuff in. When that fails, personal storage is a $22 billion industry.* Not only is that an enormous expense that stands between millions of people and their financial goals, but the excess stuff takes a toll on our mental well-being as well.

Mothers whose homes have a high density of objects are more prone to high cortisol levels and depression.† Both genders characterize the detritus in their homes as exhausting, and science has shown that the visual impact of having too many possessions can

---

* Jeanne E. Arnold, Anthony Graesch, Enzo Ragazzini, and Elinor Ochs, *Life at Home in the Twenty-First Century: 32 Families Open Their Doors* (Los Angeles: UCLA Press, 2017), 36.

† Arnold et al., *Life at Home*, 26.

lead to a sharp decrease in wellness, all from acquiring in the pursuit of happiness.

And happiness is what I am going to be bringing this conversation back to throughout this book, because that's what I care about, for you and everyone I work with. I actually don't care if your towels are put away in rainbow order. I don't need your canned goods to match. I don't need your living room to look like a Japanese temple or your paperwork to be in pretty folders. I don't care about Pinterest. I care about your well-being. I care about you being free from Clutter Blocks, because once you are, your home will support you living your fullest, most enjoyable life.

Your home is a tool that enables you to get out in the world, rested and ready for action, to live the life you want to be living. It has to work for you. If you are eating dinner in front of the TV because you are running a business you love off the dining table, great! But if you are eating in front of the TV because you're pretty sure there's a dining table over there, only no one has seen it cleared off in years, we have work to do.

People call me because there comes a tipping point. Maybe their kids have missed the bus one too many times because they can't find their homework. Maybe they've been put on notice for being late to work because getting dressed in the morning is a battle with their closet. Maybe they want to have friends over but feel embarrassed by the state of their home. In some way or other, they're not showing up how they want to be showing up, and they're not using their home how they envisioned they'd use it when they moved in. I am not telling you that how you're living doesn't meet *my* standards. You have sought me and this book out because something in your life isn't working, and by helping you figure out which Clutter Block is in your path, I will not only get it functioning for you but help you create a space you are happy to come home to.

The Brain and Clutter

In addition to all the external forces working on us to clutter our homes, there are some internal ones I want you to be aware of. Our brains evolved to have something neuroscientists call selective inattention, which is generally defined in the medical community as the screening out of stimuli that are threatening, anxiety-producing, or felt to be unimportant. We developed this way because, until the invention of guns, we were not the apex predator. We had to be constantly vigilant for bigger animals who wanted to eat us, and we adapted to stay focused on potential threats and screen out the rest. We literally don't see the majority of what's right in front of us. And the brain does it automatically. This is why people call me, suddenly freaking out about a critical clutter problem that has been developing, or simply marinating, for many years. They suddenly see it.

For example, I have a dear friend with two sons and a fairly organized home but, as I said, two sons. One day, she called me sounding like she was going to retch.

"The chair in the den is *disgusting*."

"Oh?" I asked.

"It is *covered* in food stains. It literally *stinks*. The boys have basically been using it as a giant napkin. How have I not noticed? My in-laws will be here in three hours!"

I told her to throw a quilt over it and then wait until after the weekend to set it on fire. Then I reassured her she didn't notice because the yuck happened gradually, and at some point, her brain decided it was smarter to focus on avoiding sharp LEGO pieces on the floor than look at the chair. We are all busy. We are all just trying to get from point A to point B. We don't rove our eyeballs over our homes every day with a discerning eye.

Additionally, how we keep on top of what we have has also changed rapidly in the last ten years or so. I hear from clients across all demographics, from midtwenties to mideighties, "My home didn't used to look like this." "I used to be able to keep on top of this." "I used to have the time, but I don't anymore." With video on demand and social media, clients who used to come home from work and have a few hours to kill before their program came on at 9:00 p.m., which they'd take advantage of to tidy up, can now start watching whatever they want or checking their feeds from the moment they get in the door. Putting items away and throwing them out has never been so easy to avoid. So the stuff we stop seeing piles up and becomes clutter.

Which is why we are going to be looking at your home with a fresh perspective in part 1 of this book. Brace yourself, because it can be overwhelming. I am used to standing next to people who walk me around in total shock as piles and stacks of items they've been walking by for years suddenly come into focus. But know that seeing it is the first key step to eliminating it. You're on the right track.

My Story

I grew up in the Northern California of the '70s. From a very early age, I liked my stuff organized. I had a great-aunt who was a top-selling Mary Kay saleswoman, and one of my favorite childhood memories was helping her clean out her supply closet every spring.

After college, armed with a degree in accounting, I moved to LA and fell into a series of personal assisting jobs for Hollywood professionals. I loved it because, in addition to making their lives run smoothly, I solved problems. I fixed the impossible itinerary, the leaky roof, and the IRS snafu so they could focus on whatever awesome thing they were creating. Because it isn't about your beach towels—it's about getting you to the beach.

Then in 2006, the makeup artist I was working for had a close friend whose boyfriend's tech start-up had failed. She needed me to help him dig out and shut down the business properly by ensuring all vendors were paid and everything was filed properly with the IRS. I thought...*cool*! You know how some people get really excited about squeezing pores or tweezing eyebrows and will ask everyone in the dorm if they can do theirs? I get that excited about creating order out of chaos. So I showed up the first day, sleeves rolled up, coffee in hand, ready to file, and instead found an emotional archaeological dig. I found a man who was reeling from disappointment, who was going into the office every day and just sitting, surrounded by boxes and boxes and piles and piles of forms, receipts, invoices, tax records, and company files.

He was in a total state of paralysis.

So moving around him, I just dug in. I found layers that I've now come to expect on paperwork jobs. The top layer is where everything is going off the rails: overdue invoices from vendors, letters from the IRS, and unpaid utilities. Under that is the hope and promise, the layer where things were starting to grow and looked like they'd continue on that way indefinitely: patent files, prospective leases for larger spaces, and résumés from prospective hires. And the bottom layer is usually where we find what I call the seeds of chaos. Where I discover that they didn't set up a filing system for their first payables and then couldn't get on top of it. Or there are a bunch of receipts just shoved in a drawer.

But when I pushed this guy to try to deal with any of it, he couldn't. This immediately reminded me of my dad.

My dad was a lawyer. He's smart, funny, and eccentric. He is also a hoarder.

As a kid, one of my most vivid memories is driving along the freeway in my dad's convertible Karmann Ghia and him pulling over to hang my little brother over the side to pick up a tool that was laying by the road. "That's a perfectly good tool that I might need someday," I remember him saying.

Over the years, there were other clues. The fact that my brother and I could never get a straight answer about how many cars he owned or how many storage units he paid for. He was always dragging a bag or box of paperwork with him wherever he went like he was about to do his taxes at any second. To me, it felt like his belongings, what looked like trash, always seemed to be more important to him than I was. All his energy went into collecting the stuff, managing the stuff, moving the stuff, or freaking out when someone threw the stuff away. The pain and unhappiness it has caused him gave me insight into the power our things have over us. It's not about the pile of paper; it's about what that pile represents.

As I was standing in this client's office, doing this postmortem, I had an aha moment. I started asking him questions about the business, what he'd been trying to achieve, the highs and lows. What happened over the course of those next three weeks changed both our lives. As he started talking about the start-up— what he'd done right and what had gone wrong—he gradually came back to life. He started moving around the space, helping me sort, categorize, and shred. He was able to confront the autopsy of his failure.

And I was discovering that I had a lens that was different from other organizers. Because of my dad, I intrinsically understood that clutter is an emotional issue and that the reason why we accumulate it—and why we can't let go of it—often connects with our deepest fears and sadness.

I knew by the end of our time together that I was going to shift from assisting to organizing full time.

Meanwhile, the client found a prototype in the files that he realized he had never followed through on. That was the one that worked. He is a very successful entrepreneur today. If someone had just come in and eighty-sixed everything, without giving him the opportunity to confront and process it, he would have missed that huge opportunity. It's an opportunity I give all my clients and the bedrock of what I call the dClutterfly Method.

The Emotional Clutter Blocks

If you want your home to look different than it does, but you can't seem to take any action, there is an emotional underpinning. If you think, "I should really get rid of some of this stuff," and then freeze, there is something there worth looking at. You are not lazy. You are not a "poor housekeeper." Most likely there is just a Clutter Block preventing you from taking the action you want in your heart.

I have seen over and over that once the block is identified and conquered, the same clients who couldn't free themselves from clutter are suddenly able to create order and keep it by healing the emotional need that the chaos was masking. In the next chapter, you will learn how to recognize them in yourself and—most importantly—how to break through them!

Before we get into the meat of Clutter Blocks, let me inspire you by ending this chapter with one of my favorite client stories of a major Clutter Block breakthrough that perfectly depicts what can be unleashed when a Clutter Block is released.

The first thing that struck me when I met Angela was that she was a stylish, highly successful woman with lots of responsibility on her shoulders. In addition to her high-pressure job in marketing at a top branding firm, she managed the apartment building she lived in and the care of her mentally ill mother. But the most striking thing to me was that for a person who had so many of areas of her life together, her apartment was a disaster. There were papers and unopened mail everywhere and clothes piled on every surface. In fact, there were so many clothes on her bed and the floor of her bedroom that she slept on the couch. Recently, she'd been getting in trouble at work for being late and was worried she might lose her job. She had called me so that getting ready for work in the morning became manageable again.

But as we started to excavate her clothes, I noticed that most of what was hanging in the prime spots weren't the clothes that she wore every day to work but an extensive collection of white linen resort wear.

"So," I asked, "what's with all the resort wear? Do you wear it often?"

She answered, "Well no, not often, but I will. Someday. Very soon.

Those clothes are for when I get a boyfriend and when we buy a second home in Hawaii and start spending half our time there."

When she had to keep interrupting our work to crisis-manage her ill mother, I realized Angela was trapped in Emotional Clutter Block #4: My Fantasy Stuff for My Fantasy Life. She was hanging on to never-worn clothes for "someday," because her here and now was completely emotionally overwhelming—stressful and lonely at the same time. She had a lot on her plate, and wanting to escape a little was only natural. But the problem was that the Clutter Block was coming close to sabotaging the one thing she had keeping her afloat—her job.

I said, "Your closet is a tool to help your day-to-day life run smoother. It's a not a dream catcher. Let's take a hard look at these clothes and see if (a) you will ever really wear them and (b) if there is a better place to store them."

As we started to wade through the clothes and she suddenly saw how many of the items still had tags, she began to realize the money she was wasting. She finally understood that her clutter crisis happened because she was so busy taking care of her fantasy life that she was letting her real life fall apart.

After purging a huge portion of the "vacation clothes," we were able to put her work clothes away in the closet, hung neatly so getting dressed in the morning was easy. We cleared off the bed so

she could get a good night's rest. With those things sorted, she soon got a promotion at work and with the extra money was able to hire a full-time caregiver for her mother. That freed up the time and energy for online dating, which is how she met the man she now travels with. They haven't bought a house in Hawaii yet, but once the life *inside* her apartment was setting her up for success *outside* her apartment, she was able to take the actions to make her dreams her reality.

Love is so much better than an unworn linen pantsuit.

2

the seven emotional clutter blocks: which one(s) do you have?

ON ANY GIVEN JOB, THERE COMES A MOMENT WHERE I hold up something that is empirically garbage, a grocery list from years ago, half a Popsicle stick house, or a VHS player sitting next to a DVD player sitting next to a smart TV. I move toward the garbage bag or the recycle box, and I am met with wild-eyed panic. "Oh no," my client will say. "I can't possibly get rid of that."

We've hit a block.

Every day, people who have hired me to help them get rid of their excess stuff, who are paying me *by the hour* to get rid of their excess stuff, give me reasons why they can't let go of their excess stuff.

I kept hearing the same seven reasons over and over and started to understand that when you *want* to do something but simply *can't*, there is a blockage there. Once I started being able to quickly identify which block we were working with and to codify a way to release each one, the work with my clients shifted. People were able to release the stuff that had a hold over them faster, with greater ease and lasting results.

So let's dive in, but just know, this is emotional territory. This not a breeze. This isn't the part of the process that's about using your label maker, making more space in your drawers, and posting a picture on Instagram. Looking at your Clutter Blocks requires a little personal honesty, a little vulnerability, a little accountability, and a little willingness to change.

Please know, we all have at least one. There is nothing you are going to read here that you are alone with. We all try to hold onto something some time.

Emotional Clutter Blocks: What Are They and Where Do They Come From?

We all tell ourselves stories. It's how our brains are wired to make sense of our world. We are meaning-making machines. Think of silly examples: Rain on your wedding day? You'll have a baby within the year! A pigeon poops on you? It's good luck! Those are just two crazy incidents where humans conspired to make meaning where, in fact, there is none. "Bad things happen at random" is a concept that we as a species have a *very* hard time sitting with.

So somewhere along the line, you told yourself a story about something, some object in your home, to have its presence make sense so you could stop thinking about it. You open the cupboard under the window seat, and there are all the scented candles you've ever been given. At some point, you decided that you were saving them for a special occasion. You know, one of those special occasions that can only properly be commemorated with a scented candle. Right? Say it out loud. It makes no sense. But you, and millions of people just like you, have squirrelled away smelly candles. (And bath salts, but we'll get to that.)

So you had a thought: "Let's save this for later." Over time, with enough repetition, it becomes a belief: "We save candles and nice gifts for special occasions."

Now, a few years later, the cupboard is full, you've never enjoyed a candle, most of them have lost their smell, and you have a *limiting* belief. A limiting belief is just what it sounds like—a belief you hold onto that limits you.

Add a few more years and a few more candles, and now you have a Clutter Block.

When I ask if maybe we can throw away the ones that have melted and leached their color through the cardboard, staining it pink and red, and you are horrified, you *definitely* have Clutter Block #5.

Frequently, these blocks are historical, meaning there's a family history that either created or set the stage for the block. We rarely look at the beliefs about stuff that we inherit from our parents and grandparents, but there are powerful messages there.

My mother's grandparents emigrated from Germany, and their German heritage was a huge part of their identity. To this day, my mother cannot get rid of anything she inherited that came from Germany—because that's what *her* mother instilled in her. To make sure I'm not the fourth generation with Clutter Block #6, I've taught myself what matters is if I have good memories of an object—not where it was made.

So as we go through each block, if one resonates for you, try to remember if your mother or grandmother had the same one. Often, simply having lived through the scarcity of the Depression and the world wars means that earlier generations passed along some pretty intense messages about needing to hold onto things. Remember, those maxims were created in a different time and place. Similar to the Sicilian grandmother stuffing her obese grandson full of cannoli because she grew up hungry, it's important for us to reexamine these inherited messages.

I'll give you common clues for each block to measure against your own clutter. Some clues are signs of multiple blocks, so look at each one in context and see which block is predominant for you. Think of it like WebMD. A rash could be the symptom of anything from poison ivy to Lyme disease. You have to look at the symptom in context to be able to diagnose the underlying pathology, and you may have more than one block! For example, #5 and #7 frequently go hand in hand.

Once my clients recognize which block they're up against, I give them what I call a bridge, a specific approach to tackling it that has been proven to work for hundreds of other clients. I also give them a mantra to repeat as they are defying the block with each item they take down, pack up, and give away.

CLUTTER BLOCK #1: *My Stuff Keeps Me in the Past*

When the past is taking up prime real estate in your present, it's a sign that some part of you might believe that the best times of your life are behind you. That isn't what we want your home to be reinforcing for you. Memories are wonderful, and I am all for keeping mementoes that fill you with positive emotions when you pass them, but what I often find with clients is that over time, the feelings those possessions elicit have shifted, and they haven't noticed.

For example, I have a client whose mother, Grace, was a very successful ballerina in the '50s and '60s, and she had wallpapered the entire central stairwell of their home with framed press clippings and PR photos of her in her glory days. The problem was that Grace had started putting those photos up when she was still dancing—they commemorated each achievement, and walking past them each night on her way to bed from a performance filled her with a sense of triumph. Thirty years later, however, her daughter finally got her to admit, they actually made her sad. They filled her with a sense of loss—of her abilities, of everyone she had worked with who had died of AIDS, and of time. Every time she went from one floor to another, she was unconsciously bumming herself out a little bit. And that had started to take a toll on her mental health. Once vivacious, she had become withdrawn.

At my suggestion, her daughter proposed an experiment. She knew it would be too much for Grace to see the pictures come down at home, so she suggested to her mother that she allow her to take down the same kind of photos in her summer home and see how it felt for two months.

Well, Grace did not go gracefully into this experiment. She was as mad as a nest of hornets, but something amazing happened that summer. Over the course of the weeks, she had more energy than she'd reported in years, and she reached out to more friends and made more plans. The week before she was scheduled to come back to the city, she asked her daughter if she could take down the majority of the photos at home and have the stairwell repainted before her return.

Grace started teaching ballet again, and the last years of her life were some of her busiest and happiest.

So if you have a glory wall, what emotions do these items really bring up for you? Too often, I find that what started as a celebration has morphed into nostalgia for long-gone yesterdays. If all the items are commemorating events over a decade past, it's time to shake things up.

The Clues

When I'm touring through someone's home, here are a few of the things I see that tip me off that we may be facing Clutter Block #1, My Stuff Keeps Me in the Past:

* Large amounts of children's artwork (but no more children)
* Trophies and awards from years long past
* Outdated clothes that no longer fit the time or the person
* A glory wall of photos or articles framed and blown up
* All the dishes to host a holiday they don't host anymore
* Tools in the garage for making repairs they can't make anymore

None of these is a block on its own. They are only blocks if these items are taking up space with the past, preventing you from getting curious about today or tomorrow, or if looking at these items reinforces the idea that your best days are behind you.

Because none of us knows that. Grace couldn't have foreseen that she'd start teaching.

I want your home to be setting you up to be in a place of curiosity about today and the future. If it feels like a museum of *then*, you're shortchanging your *now*.

The Bridge

Is hanging on to this item in alignment with your vision for your life right now? Allow yourself to acknowledge and experience any feelings of loss that come up. It's important to remember that the stuff can't actually keep the past alive. Then give yourself permission to hold onto one box of the items that represent that time, place, or age for you. Care for it properly, meaning don't put it in the basement if it's damp, and don't put it in the attic if you have mice. Make sure this is something that future generations can look through and immediately understand the story you were trying to tell.

The Helpful Phrase

Say or think as often as you need to:

"Letting go of this old stuff makes space for the life I want now."

I have some clients who walk around muttering the phrase under their breath for the entire day. It helps keep their eyes on the prize and reinforces the goal.

CLUTTER BLOCK #2: *My Stuff Tells Me Who I Am*

Helen was a retired fund-raiser. In her career, she had helped thousands of people get access to health care they may not otherwise have had. She started mental health clinics in poor neighborhoods while raising three fantastic boys. But stuff was always her release valve, her mental go-to. She'd hit TJ Maxx or the Christmas Tree Shops on the way home from work, and she always had a running dialogue about her purchases. *I've been looking for a purse this shade of green to match that skirt I got last year!* So the purchase didn't fill her with anxiety but with a sense of accomplishment. She wasn't shopping; she was problem-solving.

But when I met her, she lived alone. Her grown sons were in other parts of the country, and her days were quiet. So what did she do now that she was on a fixed income? She went to Walgreens or CVS or the gas station several times a day. She'd buy gum or antacids or shampoo. And she'd talk to the salespeople. For a few minutes, she held their undivided attention.

I have seen women do the same thing on Rodeo Drive. While they are debating a purchase, they are in the driver's seat, and it gives them a sense of power. They are fawned over and flattered.

Empirically, there is nothing wrong with this; we all enjoy it from time to time. But if this is a *daily* habit for you, I want you to ask yourself: Why do I need these things? What am I looking to them to tell me about myself? That I'm successful? That I'm loved? That's a big burden to put on an inanimate object.

I don't care if you have three hundred pairs of jeans, as long as you know that you, naked, in an empty room, are someone worthy of respect and love. Do it right now. Close your eyes and imagine you are standing naked in an empty room. Who are you? What do you bring to the party? It can't be your watch or your heels.

What makes you awesome is happening between your ears and under your rib cage. If hearing that feels very uncomfortable for you, then this might be your block.

The Clues

When I go into a client's house who has this Clutter Block #2, My Stuff Tells Me Who I Am, I tend to see:

◆   Boxes in the entry, evidence of excessive online shopping

- Shopping bags with purchases that were never even unpacked
- Clothes hanging in the closet with tags on them
- Multiples of items
- Brand flaunting or bargain flaunting or both

The Bridge

Here is what I am going to challenge you to do: create daily meaningful interactions that are not transactional, that don't cost you anything or bring anything into your home. One wonderful way is to be of service. There are endless organizations that need helping hands.

Helen took all her fund-raising acumen and started volunteering to help local nonprofits with their grant writing and outreach. It helped her meet people who valued her smarts and skills and reminded her that she had more to offer than her appearance—or buying power.

The Helpful Phrase

Say or think:

"I can meaningfully connect with people without acquiring anything.

In fact, I am a valuable person without any possessions at all."

It may not feel true for you right away, but that disconnect is what prompts you to try to make it true, which will shift your belief.

CLUTTER BLOCK #3: *The Stuff I'm Avoiding*

When I met Christopher, he was forty-two years old and had hired me to come by and do a simple paperwork-organizing project. But in going through the stacks stashed all around his house, I noticed a huge amount of correspondence from the IRS. Most of it was unopened and went back at least five years. I asked Chris why he hadn't dealt with it, and the floodgates opened. He'd made a bad choice when closing his last company, and now he owed the government money. He was afraid to find out how much, because he had finally fallen in love with an amazing woman he wanted to marry. "How can I propose to her with this huge secret?" he asked.

I encouraged him to go see a top tax lawyer and accountant. When he took them his (now neatly organized) paperwork, they found that Chris didn't owe nearly as much as he'd feared. He created a payment plan that worked for him, and last I saw on Facebook, he'd proposed, and they look very happy together.

This block, possibly more than any other, is poisonous, because while you're avoiding the thing you're afraid of, you're creating tremendous anxiety for yourself. Chris's head-in-the-sand approach to his money problems nearly cost him much more than cash: it could have cost him the love of his life.

I don't know why so many people suffer from the magical

thinking that the contents of an unopened envelope or an unopened email don't really exist, but I see more of this than you would believe. I also see half-finished home-improvement projects, donations sitting in the dining room, boxes blocking the garage that were supposed to be removed months—or years—ago. I say this to you now: it will not take care of itself, and you are undermining your self-confidence with every day that goes by and you don't act.

So if you have items that you have been avoiding dealing with, know that we can tackle them together. With support from me and your friends and family, we will vanquish the block and the actual stuff clogging up your home, piece by piece.

And then we'll help you put simple strategies in place to make sure it never builds up to this scary, overwhelming place again.

The Clues

I know we're up against Clutter Block #3, The Stuff I'm Avoiding, when I tour a client's home and see a lot of:

- Unfiled paperwork
- Unopened mail
- Unfinished projects
- Unreturned items
- A large to-do pile or list

The Bridge

There is no magic bullet. If this is paper clutter you've been avoiding, invite someone over to support you, get out your shredder, and start opening. Whether you end up needing debt consolidation help, a tax payment plan, or you actually find money in the pile (my clients find money all the time), the opportunity is here for you to live your life differently moving forward. There is very little information that can come in a corporate envelope that has the power to derail your entire life. It's time to put that fear to bed.

I find what can be really helpful with some clients is asking them point-blank: What are you so afraid of?

I'll owe money. I'll lose my house. I'll lose my insurance.

"Okay," I'll say. "Now, play it through. Finish the sentence." Meaning, if you owe money to the IRS—or anyone—you will set up a payment plan and take care of it. If you have to sell your house, then you will use that equity you have smartly been accruing in your home to put everything to rights and find a new place you will also enjoy. If you missed a premium payment, pick a new insurer. Whatever it is, it can be handled. In all my years of excavating paperwork with clients, not a single person, no matter their age or situation, has found anything they couldn't deal with.

If it's endless half-finished projects you've been avoiding, now is the time to unstick your life by tackling them. Maybe you are never going to make a wedding album. Maybe this is a favor you ask your newly retired mom. Maybe you hire someone to finish repainting your den. Whatever it requires, get it *done*. It will give your life a boost of momentum that will feel *so* good.

The Helpful Phrase

I encourage my clients to repeat:

"I have power over my papers. They have no power over me."

Or if they've been avoiding dealing with their projects:

"Done is better than perfect."

Because it's true. You are a strong, capable person. There is *nothing* in there you can't handle. Start proving it to yourself. You are going to be so proud once you confront whatever it is you're avoiding. So don't put that feeling off another day. It's yours for the taking.

CLUTTER BLOCK #4: *My Fantasy Stuff for My Fantasy Life*
Remember Angela with the apartment full of unworn resort wear? She was a quintessential #4.

Then there was my client Kay, who was morbidly obese. In her aspirations to eat better, she had bought every conceivable high-end gadget to make healthy meals. She figured that if she spent so much money, she would definitely *use* them and attain her goals.

Of course, instead, she found the mess so overwhelming, she never cooked. She ordered in and always ended up eating off her plan.

So we purged it all. The KitchenAid stand mixer with the spiralizing attachment, the NutriBullet, which sat next to the Vitamix, the Cuisinart Pro, the device for shrink-wrapping your own chicken breasts, the rice cooker and the slow cooker and the Instant Pot. It all went away! We pared her down to a few simple items, and she started preparing her own food and eventually lost weight.

If you are holding on to an overabundance of items for "someday," they are telling you that you have stopped investing in the now. Interestingly, I have seen a sharp uptick in this ever since *The Secret*, especially among my female clients. Women tend to think that somehow buying an item is showing the universe that they are committed to their goal. So the woman trying to get pregnant has already bought maternity wear and the baby clothes; the dieter buys clothes six sizes too small; the single woman buys an eighty-inch TV to attract the man who will someday move in with her. Yes, I have seen all this—multiple times.

We use shopping as a shorthand for doing the work. There was a great episode of *The Golden Girls* where Dorothy discovers that her eighty-something-year-old mother has been bulk shopping. When confronted, Sophia answers, "You get twenty cases of sardines, you figure: God doesn't want me to waste good sardines. He's gonna wait till I finish the twenty cases. That could take five, six years." It's funny—and poignant and true. We imbue objects with tremendous power.

We dress for the job we want, not the job we have. We have lucky socks and lucky mitts and lucky helmets. We put our pajamas on backward when we want a snow day and think that we are one new lip gloss away from *everything* changing.

All of us use possessions as talismans against vulnerability. But I don't want them to take over your house or become an obstacle to the life you really want to be living.

The Clues

I know I'm looking at Clutter Block #4, My Fantasy Stuff for My Fantasy Life, when I see:

* Lots of items that have never been used
* Clothes with their tags on
* Appliances in boxes
* Exercise equipment that's never been assembled
* A disconnect between the merchandise and the life

The Bridge

Ultimately, our lives are not a Disney movie, and the teapot can't make the tea for us. Boxing gloves don't make us box, and the stuff we acquire doesn't change our behavior. I would encourage you to think about *action* instead of *acquisition*.

What is more important: getting all new workout gear or showing up to the class in any old thing but actually *taking the class*? What can you do today to move yourself closer to your dream? Otherwise, the stuff you bought to manifest your dream will become the obstacle.

The Helpful Phrase

I encourage my clients to repeat:

"Stuff will not get me there. Action will get me there."

When clients are donating the unused items, they shouldn't feel as if they're giving up on their dreams. The opposite is true! They are shedding the stuff that was weighing the dream down! It feels so good to no longer be burdened by things that are languishing in your life. Over and over, I have seen that once my clients stop buttressing themselves behind items that are actually a *rebuke* to them in their disuse, they are freed up to do something that moves them genuinely closer to happiness.

And remember, *that's* what I care most about: your happiness.

CLUTTER BLOCK #5: *I'm Not Worth My Good Stuff*

Are you holding onto fancy things, linens, glasses, or clothes that are in reserve for "someday"? Are you using items that are thread-bare, broken, stained while the good stuff languishes?

A Japanese-American couple in their seventies hired me at the *strong* suggestion of their son to help them downsize. It wasn't an enormous challenge, because they had—and used—very few objects. Everything had been bought at Marshalls, and much of it was chipped or stained, fairly dreary and depressing. I was helping them pare down to the best of the selection and getting it all packed when I discovered an armoire packed full of unopened boxes, wrapped in gorgeous kimono-patterned paper and tied with crumbling ribbon.

"What are these?" I asked.

"Oh," the wife said. "Don't worry about those. We'll take them."

"Yes, but what *are* they?" It was like a dream or a children's story, finding a secret cupboard full of gifts.

"Those are our wedding presents."

I tried to do some quick math. Her daughter had mentioned nothing on the phone that sounded like there was divorce or second marriages. "When were you married?"

"1972."

"Mrs. Sato, we need to open these. There's no point in taking things if they're no longer useful."

She nodded and agreed that the time had come—forty years later—to open the boxes.

What we found was astounding. Sumptuous linens, gorgeous crystal glasses, and koi-patterned porcelain. "Oh, Mrs. Sato, why didn't you use these? They're so beautiful."

"They're too nice," she said. "We don't live like this."

But they could have.

The Clues

I have a fairly good idea that we are bumping up against Clutter Block #5, I'm Not Worth My Good Stuff, when I see:

- A closet full of designer clothes, but my client only wears sweatpants or leggings
- Unlit candles, unused bath salts, packed away china, packed away silver
- Clients using the phrase, "I'm saving that..." When for?

The Bridge

Challenge yourself to start using anything you've been saving. Have people over! Or don't. Set the table with the good china for yourself! More and more of my clients are using their inherited "good" silver for everyday flatware. So maybe it isn't polished to the point you can see your reflection in the knife, but hey, we don't live in Downton Abbey, so no one is keeping track of how shiny your flatware is. Use the silver and love it!

The Helpful Phrase

A friend of mine's mother died last year after a long battle with cancer. After she passed, her daughter was cleaning out under the bathroom sink and found years' worth of unopened gifts for a woman confined to her bed, luxury hand and foot lotions, beautiful candles, bath salts—all of it turned, all of it now just sour-smelling garbage. She posted a picture of it on Facebook with an exhortation to her friends that I would encourage you to say to yourself:

"Use the good stuff! Today is worth celebrating!"

I want you to believe that about your life. Today is worthy of the good soap, the good towels, the tube of truffle paste. Because you deserve them, and if you don't use them, you will waste them. And both are a huge shame.

CLUTTER BLOCK #6: *Trapped with Other People's Stuff* ·
Nora hired me because she was living in a museum. She was the sixth generation of her family to live in her Cobble Hill brownstone, a rarity in New York, and she loved the history—but hated the clutter. She needed me to talk her father into some desperately

needed editing. The top three floors were filled with hundreds of trunks of parasols, opera programs from the early 1900s, receipts from butcher shops and grocery stores, etc. No one in their family had ever thrown anything away. It was all interesting and historical, but keeping it all meant that Nora and her husband were paying property taxes on a home they couldn't actually use. And with a baby on the way, things had to change.

When her father arrived to help, he was aghast. He immediately started moving stuff back from the donate pile to the keep pile. Nora told him everything interesting would be donated to the New York Historical Society or to the theater program at Juilliard, but he had been born in the parlor of the house, and the idea of parting with anything panicked him.

"We don't know what's valuable. This furniture is old—it's worth a fortune! My great-aunt left me that tureen—we have to keep it!" The problem was the furniture, with its disintegrating silk and old-fashioned style, actually had no resale value anymore, and Nora wasn't about to use that tureen or anything else he was insisting had to stay. He was in the grips of Clutter Block #6.

Finally, I sat him down and said, "Here is what Nora wants. To raise her baby in this house and carry on that family tradition. She wants to stay near you so that you are in this baby's life every day, but if we don't clear this stuff out so she can modernize and babyproof, she will move to Seattle. Which do you want more: your grandchild or the tureen?"

It took a few rounds over a few months, but her father was able to break through his Clutter Block and even liked how the place looked so much, he had me over to *his* house a few blocks away to start clearing out his memorabilia.

So often, when we go to donate an inherited item that isn't used—or even really liked—I'll be told that, according to family lore, the object is valuable, so no dice. I call this the *Antiques Roadshow* mentality. Everyone is convinced that old cookie jar or water-stained *Winnie-the-Pooh* print is their lottery ticket. But are you sure? I always recommend pulling up the item on eBay to see what it's actually sold for in the past. It might be pennies.

Across the board, the market for Victorian antiques has died. Now everyone wants midcentury modern. That ornate breakfront of your great-grandparents that your mother lovingly cared for might actually have had a strong resale value in the '80s, but it doesn't anymore. So when some hipster wants to take it off your hands, paint it Day-Glo pink, and give it a whole next life, let them.

Frequently, a client will say to me or their spouse that they should take these treasured items to the "other" house. You know, the house they inherited from a parent or in-law that they are in the process of cleaning out. And have been for the previous five, six, seven years!

What happens is that at some point in their fifties or sixties, they inherit an entire packed house and can't deal. There's no mortgage and nominal taxes, so they just keep it. And then they move *their* excess stuff over. It's like being able to store fat on someone else's body.

So now they have a mausoleum that needs clearing that they're filling with their own inability to make a decision. They are compounding a Clutter Block on top of a Clutter Block!

Don't do it! Why? Because your time isn't limitless either, and it's not kind to leave a mess. Don't punt those decisions down the line.

Clients also frequently say to me, "This has been passed down for so long, how can I be the one to let go of it?" Well, because it's now yours—yours to store, yours to clean, yours to move. You have every right to unburden yourself of that, and the fact is that if you are feeling this way about the object, your children aren't going to be *more* enthusiastic about it. Let it go.

The Clues

There is a strong chance we are looking at Clutter Block #6, Trapped with Other People's Stuff, if I see:

- Four sets of china
- Mismatched Victorian furniture lining a room, two breakfronts, multiple secretaries, and hutches
- Excessive antiques
- Boxes of memorabilia
- Boxes of unlabeled photographs
- Unused rooms of uncomfortable inherited beds or couches that no one sleeps/sits on

The Bridge

Just because this piece of furniture or this collection of horseshoes was important to someone else doesn't mean it has to be important to you. Think about that person. Do you eat the same food? Do you wear their clothes? If you do not, then you shouldn't have to live with something just because it was theirs. You are different people living your prime in different decades with different needs and demands. I am giving you permission to respect and honor yours.

Another important truth—and this can feel hard to process for someone grieving—is that the items you keep of someone who's passed away do not prove how much you love them. I adored my late grandmother, but I have very few items of hers. One item I have kept is a very old leather satchel that she used to carry every day. It's completely useless to me but it hangs with my other purses, and every time I see it, I think of her and smile from ear to ear.

On that same note, being respectful to their memory does not mean you have to guard all their possessions for the rest of your life. You're not honoring your family's memories by living in a storage unit, and you can't help it if tastes have changed. You have the right to live in your own here and now. So let me suggest a few ways to celebrate them without their stuff. Make their favorite recipe on their birthday. Plant a tree or donate to get a bench in your local park in their honor. Hang their picture somewhere you'll see every day. Do something along those lines, and let go of the breakfront.

The Helpful Phrase

Think or say:

"I can love and hold their memory and still let go of their things."

This goes back to the magic we imbue objects with that we talked about with Clutter Block #4, and there is something wonderful about touching something that a loved one touched in their life. So pick the handful that give you those feels, and let the rest go. The items you choose to keep will feel even more special and potent for being rare.

CLUTTER BLOCK #7: *The Stuff I Keep Paying For*

After I split up with an ex, I bought a pair of pants.

I think you can picture the scene: I'm ridiculously skinny from being emotionally wrung-out, I'm emotionally vulnerable because I just want someone, anyone, to tell me everything is going to be okay, and I want to transform one more day of packing and crying into something *fabulous*.

They were black with a pattern of little white skulls. And they cost a fortune.

I wore them exactly once and then finally resumed sleeping and eating normally, and they never fit again. This wasn't, like, oh, if I gave up bread for a week, they would fit. It was I would need someone to marry and divorce me all over again for these to fit.

So they hung in my closet. Month in, month out. As my business was getting busier and busier, I was opening the closet every day, and it was like those pants were laughing at me. "You tell people to get rid of things they can't use all day long, and yet we've been hanging here for three years?"

But I would think, "Four hundred dollars." I can't. I just can't.

Until one day, I just realized I had to take my own medicine, and it was a brutal pill to swallow. I put them in a bag and took them to Covenant House, which houses and clothes homeless teens, and dropped them off.

Two weeks later, I saw a sixteen-year-old girl in my pants going into her job at the yogurt shop. Through volunteering at the organization, I later found out that she had been sex-trafficked since she was ten years old. The pants were part of a mini wardrobe they put together for her so she could get a job and start studying for her GED.

Those pants could have spent the rest of their life in my closet, so I didn't "make a mistake" in buying them, or they could give someone a little boost where they'd had none.

The Clues

Clutter Block #7, The Stuff I Keep Paying For, is harder to spot, but it's easier to hear:

- "But I paid a lot for that."
- "I don't want it to go to waste."
- "I might use it."
- "That could be useful."

The Bridge

Breaking through Clutter Block #7 is very much about self-acceptance. To quote Big Bird, "Everyone makes mistakes, oh yes they do." We are being marketed at *all day long*. We are going to succumb sometimes, and that means we are going to buy items that we ultimately don't use. Please don't keep that item out of fear of confronting the slip-up.

When you buy something, you are just making a good guess. You *think* it's something you're going to reach for in your closet, but you can't know for sure, because that decision is going to be made by your future self, and you can't know how he or she will be feeling.

Instead of thinking of buying the item, think of buying the option of that item. It's in your closet or your fridge, so you can have the option of it if you so choose. If, over however long you owned it, you haven't exercised that option, pass it along so someone else can have it.

If this is your block, you will most likely have a moment where you are confronted with the cost of your clutter. This could mean adding up storage fees you've been turning a blind eye to or simply adding up what you've spent on items you've never used.

Sitting with this is an important part of the process. Almost every client at some point has a gut punch of how much money they've wasted. Even me. Don't let it trip you into a new shame spiral. But sit with it.

And let it stop here.

What is your time and mental health worth? If something is unused, you're still wasting it. Let it move on to someone who can get good use out of it.

The Helpful Phrase

Think or say:

"It's okay that I made a mistake. My home is not an orphanage for unused objects. I can let this go to someone who will actually use it or even to the garbage, and I am still a good person."

And don't throw good money after bad by continuing to store items that aren't getting used. Forgive yourself and move on.

Practical Tips for Releasing a Block

Now that we've gone through each Clutter Block, I want to offer you a few resources to help you release these blocks if they prove tenacious or bring up larger issues that are asking for your love and attention.

First, frequently just identifying a block is hugely liberating. *Oh, I'm not some weird candle hoarder! I just have trouble letting myself use the good stuff!* Just that awareness could be enough to open those jars of truffle sauce your boss gave you last Christmas that you've been saving.

But if the next time someone gives you a gift, your instinct is to put it away, still in its tissue paper, talk it through with a friend—or a therapist. Journaling can also be very therapeutic. If you have #5 (I'm Not Worth My Good Stuff), for example, you could ask yourself: What feeling does using nice things bring up? What is the feeling associated with holding onto them?

Once you've increased your awareness about what it feels like to hold onto something, you can start to consciously work with releasing that feeling. Meditation has been proven extremely effective for that, even just five minutes a day. There are endless apps now to help you start to build a habit. As you develop awareness that the feeling is created by the thoughts your brain is choosing, you'll build mental muscles around choosing other thoughts.

In the resources section, I have listed some other therapeutic methods my clients have found hugely helpful for staying present and vanquishing Clutter Blocks as they arise. They include the Sedona Method, cognitive behavioral therapy, and emotional freedom techniques (EFT), or tapping, as it is popularly known. Please investigate further, and find one that works for you.

Ultimately, understanding these blocks and being able to recognize them in yourself is empowering. It's all just useful information that will help you do all the fantastic clearing work in part 2. So don't freak out if you have one or two or more. It just means you've come to the right place.

3

how to listen to your clutter, room by room

I'D LIKE YOU TO CONSIDER A RADICAL IDEA THAT GOES TO the heart of what I believe to be true about clutter: it's not random. It doesn't happen by accident. Even the soccer ball on the dining table, you *chose* that. Why?

No, I genuinely mean it: *Why?*

Asking this question is what separates me from my professional peers. I strongly believe that taking the time to ask yourself why *this* clutter is in *this* place is how you ensure that it doesn't come back. In my experience, there are patterns to clutter, like tea leaves, and they can be read to reveal Clutter Blocks. The number one mistake people make when creating a clear path is bagging everything up and tossing it out without ever stopping and asking the clutter what it had to tell to you about changes that need to be made. Without those changes, without addressing the emotional root of clutter, it will just come back.

Think of it like this: you could have lower back pain. You take ibuprofen and make it go away. But when the ibuprofen wears off, the pain comes back. If, instead, you addressed the reason for the pain—starting with the assumption that the pain is trying to tell you something—then maybe instead you'd see a chiropractor, get a better mattress, or start bending at your knees, and the pain would go away for good. That is my approach: delve into the underlying Clutter Block to heal it forever.

There is no judgment here. I am just asking you to consider whether some changes in these areas might inspire you to free up some space in your mind and life, empowering you to live the way you imagined you would the day you moved in.

Two big clues that there might be something emotional under your clutter are:

1. If you're a repeat offender. Did your niece help you clean out your garage last year? Does it now look like she was never there?
2. If you create systems for yourself but can't maintain them. Did you make a filing system, but everything is on your desk? Did you reorganize your closet but still get dressed out of the laundry hamper?

In this chapter, I'm going to take you through my clients' homes room by room and tell you what I typically see as clutter asking for attention or change. Then we'll take a tour of your home.

If this starts to feel stressful or brings up Clutter Blocks, don't worry—I've got you. I am coming with you to help you see what you may have been trying to ignore for quite some time. Here's what I mean by that. Think back to Angela. What those piles of clothes were telling her was that what she *needed* was more help with her mother, so she didn't escape into a fantasy of someday through shopping. By paying attention to what she was doing, she healed her Clutter Block and freed up money for her mother's care, which enabled her career to take off.

So bear with me. There is a potential here for a really valuable exploration of your clutter.

The Tour

Show me everything.

That's the first thing I say to clients—and I mean it.

After helping people put their homes and lives in order for the last decade, I honestly think the number one thing that keeps people stuck in an overcrowded space is *shame*. Embarrassment. However, you can't embarrass me. There is nothing I haven't seen.

Whatever you have stuffed in your closet, shower, garage, or pantry, please know you are not alone.

Entryway

The first thing I pay attention to is if an entryway says, "Welcome to my home" or "Welcome to my to-do list." While the entryway is a great place to put the stuff you are imminently taking out with you—the dry cleaning, the package to be returned—the key word is *imminently*. This is not the place for those "on-their-way-out, on-their-way-in" projects, because that means every time you walk in your front door, the first thing you will feel is overwhelmed. That isn't setting you up for relaxing at-home time.

If your entryway is lined with UPS boxes, you might have Clutter Block #4, My Fantasy Stuff for My Fantasy Life. If you have cartons and cartons of files or projects you've been avoiding, it could be #3, The Stuff I'm Avoiding. If I see an odd assortment of inefficient old furniture, I know we're looking at #6, Trapped with Other People's Stuff.

This is also where I see benches buried in out-of-season coats, wall hooks coming loose because they're holding three more purses than they were made for, and console tables sagging under bags of errands never run.

This is the last place where you are before you leave for the

day and the first where you can let your shoulders drop at the end. Anything in this space that isn't serving your coming and going shouldn't be here.

Lisa and her husband were each other's second marriages, and both had a daughter the same age but with markedly different temperaments and schedules. Because they were each there only half the week, they each had a nanny to help them with the transition. The problem for Lisa was that the front hall now looked like it had been tossed by the feds. There was sporting equipment, soccer balls, ballet uniforms, library books, and backpacks. Homework was going back with the wrong girl. They were showing up at practice without their gear. There was constant fighting about whose fault it was, and quite frankly, it was a mess.

When I asked Lisa why this was the place where everything was living, she said, "Well, Janey does it this way at her mother's home, so her nanny wants it like this." As she said it aloud, she realized that, in an effort to be differential and inclusive, essentially avoiding confronting the ex-wife and nanny, she was allowing two different organizational systems to jockey for supremacy. She had Clutter Block #3, and it wasn't working for anyone.

"How do *you* want this?" I asked. "Janey can have it however she likes on the nights she's with her mother, but this is *your* home."

Lisa admitted that she wanted labeled bins for each girl's gear that lived in their room, not the hallway. Additionally, it was going to be their responsibility to get anything into their backpacks before school.

"I don't care if her sitter wants to grab and go. All this crap can't live here!" By taking the reins again and laying out one system, both girls blossomed in their responsibility, and no one took anyone else's stuff by accident anymore. The fighting stopped, and by confronting what she'd been avoiding, Lisa felt like she'd finally taken her place as the head of this new household.

So if your entryway is chaotic, it may be asking you for some better time management and for you to be the pack leader of your domicile.

Living Room

When I see a cluttered living room, it tells me we are most likely at maximum density in the rest of the house. And please don't think it's uncommon. I frequently see corners stacked with reused Trader Joe's bags packed with donations that never made it out of the house, hockey sticks on the couch, a coffee table buried under old magazines, canned goods on the mantle, old art projects on the sideboard. So often, people essentially crowd themselves out of their own living rooms with clutter! This is where we're supposed to *live*. If we can't live in it, then our home is begging for help.

What I ask clients to consider is why did they want to lock themselves out of being able to gather as a family or have other families over? Some underlying family systems work usually needs to be addressed. Sometimes this is where Clutter Block #6 comes up—the inherited furniture in this room is so impractical, it drives everyone out. Sometimes this room is so packed with shopping bags and Limoges and Lladró and Delft that I know we have some work to do on Clutter Block #2 to get down to a serene space that doesn't need to advertise this person's status to the world.

TV Room

Frequently, what I see here are old pastimes: games the kids have outgrown, puzzles you've finished, detritus from old hobbies like the war figurines or crafting supplies. This can also be the graveyard of technology: a Wii, plus a Nintendo, plus an Xbox, next to a VHS, a DVD player, a cable box, and a streaming device. And don't even get me started on remotes to devices that are long gone. Every home has at least one.

I had a client, Kristi, whose husband had kept three old, deep TV sets, sitting on the floor directly under his flat screen. When I tried to recycle them, he protested, "I can sell these. Poor people will want these TVs."

"No," I said gently. "Even poor people have flat screens."

It was classic Clutter Block #7, but the sets had served their purpose, and now it was time to take them to the e-waste center. It wasn't being wasteful; it was being respectful of the living space his wife was trying to create for them.

It's time to get very honest with yourself about whether the item has real reusable value to anyone right now, this year, this *month*. Don't be upset if the answer is no. Time marches on, and no one wants typewriter ribbons or fax paper or a Walkman anymore—all of which I see at least once a month.

Prioritize yourself and your downtime. The hours spent in this room at the end of the day are yours to relax and unwind. Whether you are reading a book or watching Netflix, have that time in a space that supports you.

Dining Room

So often people, treat this room as an extension of the garage, with towers of boxes or plastic bins stuffed in the corner—as if there was an invisibility cloak over them. This is a big repository of Clutter Block #3 because frequently, whatever people cannot confront they avoid by shoving in the room used the least. A crowded dining table tells me two things. First, that storage places are full. The Christmas wreath is on the table because the closet is holding other stuff. I'll get to this in depth at the end of the chapter, but for a start, look at what is on your table, and ask yourself why it can't go where it should live. The second is that I have yet to meet a family who has crowded out their eating area and is not going through some kind of turmoil. Whatever the issue, something isn't functioning optimally when the family isn't eating together, be it in the kitchen or the dining room, so my clients have unconsciously made it impossible for that to happen. The kids eat in front of the TV, Mom eats standing up in the kitchen, and Dad takes his out to the garage. Family counseling, couples' counseling, even divorce are all options that are far preferable to living in uncomfortable, even toxic, silence and disconnect.

Ed was a divorced father of two whose children blamed him for the split. Though he craved his nights with them, he was also ashamed of his tiny apartment and the fallout they felt from the divorce. So he shrunk from their hostility and, as a result, had turned the dining table into a staging area for his work and their stuff and let them take dinner to their rooms while he ate alone at the counter.

He called me in because he wanted to make some bright and cheerful places for the kids to keep things when they were over, bins and hooks and homework stations. I asked him about the table.

"Oh, they don't want to eat with me."

"They're kids. Let's not give them too much power. First, we're going to make it possible, and let's see where it goes from there."

He started insisting they spend at least twenty minutes eating together on their newly cleared table. It wasn't an instant slam dunk, but within a couple of weeks, they found a rhythm as a new threesome, and eventually, those dinners were the best part of their evenings together.

I live alone. Very happily most of the time, but there are inevitable windows, around my birthday or the holidays, where I can get lonely. Here is my bad habit: I always know I'm in a funk, because suddenly I have covered my dining table in piles of paperwork and a basket of laundry to be folded, because I don't want to be reminded that I'm eating alone. I am literally trying to hide the problem from myself. So I push myself to clear off a space for eating again, and I go buy some fresh flowers, and I remind myself that *my* meals and how I nourish *myself* is important and worthy of sitting down at the table, even if it's with a good book and not another person.

Kitchen

I think of kitchens like NASA. This is ground control. Your kitchen is the hub of your home, and if it's not well organized and functional, how can it launch you out into your day?

All too frequently, I see counters so packed, there isn't even room for a carrot, let alone meal prep. Valuable counter space is taken up with a Vitamix and the NutriBullet, a Crock-Pot, *and* the Instant Pot. If your counter is packed full of projects and papers and piles, you're creating distraction. What are you distracting yourself from? Do you want to be eating healthy but order in?

Is there a lot of nonkitchen stuff on your counters? I mean laundry and paperwork and the Draino that should really be under the sink?

In the pantry, check for overcrowded shelves from repeat buying or stocking food you don't actually want to eat. I can't tell you, working in LA, how many bags of mung beans, lentils, legumes, and other assorted health foods we have taken and donated to food pantries. So often, people shop with one set of intentions but cook with another. If you have a judgmental pantry full of stuff you don't actually want to eat, it might be time to make some peace with what makes you happy.

I also see people who got into the habit of bulk shopping but forgot to break it after their kids moved out. It takes a while to process that the household is down by one or a few adult bodies. I once asked a woman what was up with all the canned pineapple taking up an entire cupboard. "Oh, my son eats it while he studies. Something about the bromelain." Only he had left for college two years prior, and that pineapple wasn't getting any fresher.

This can dovetail with Clutter Block #1. Does seeing the pineapple make her feel closer to him or sad about his departure? Depending on where you are with this phase of empty nesting, it might be time to start divesting your home of some of their needs. I'm not saying no pineapple, just maybe two cans, not twenty.

Office

A cluttered office is quintessential Clutter Block #3. Clients frequently have very tidy homes, but this little corner is packed with old bills, invoices, receipts, manuals, tax returns, mail, catalogues, medical forms, insurance forms, and mailing supplies. Invariably, this means some kind of financial disarray.

Randy brought me in because her home office was making her crazy. It was piled with unopened mail, including letters about back taxes from the IRS and unpaid bills that had been sent to collections. The fear of what was happening in those envelopes kept her working long hours away from her young daughter, a situation that made her miserable.

But once we started opening all the mail and getting a handle on it,

we actually discovered enough undeposited checks to cover what she owed. So we laid it all out on the floor, the checks and the bills, so she could look at it, at what the chaos was trying to tell her. On day three of working with her, her shoulders slumped, and she teared up. "I feel guilty about being a working mom. So I wonder if I create all this unnecessary financial chaos so that I *have* to work, and it makes me feel less guilty. But, you know, also sick and terrified all the time. Which means the time I do spend with my daughter, I'm not really present."

Moving forward, she got into counseling to give herself permission to succeed, and she stopped needing money problems to justify her ambition.

If finances are your Achilles' heel, the good news is that there are more resources than ever to bring that stuff under control. What never works is avoidance. In this case, the disarray is telling you that it's time to put your big girl pants on and deal with your money.

Master Bedroom

One of my clients, Darcy, comes from a music industry family. She had a very tumultuous childhood, which turned into a wild young adulthood. In her forties, she was going back to school and wanted to turn her living room from a party space into a place she could study and think. The problem was the coffee table was covered with bedside table items, tissues, lotions, books, glasses, and cough drops. The couch was covered in bedding, and the room had clothes everywhere, because she was frequently getting ready for bed in it.

"What's happening in your bedroom?" I asked.

"Nothing," she said. "I'm just not crazy about the bed."

So we went upstairs. In the middle of her room was this little brass bed. It was bigger than a single but smaller than a double. I started to make it and realized that the sheets didn't really fit. The bed was so old that mattresses are no longer made in that size. She was sleeping on an original sixty-year-old horsehair mattress.

She admitted, "My head blows up from dust allergies, but it was my mom's from when she was little." I realized she was in the grips of Clutter Block #6. She was holding on to her late mother's bed because she had never really connected with her in childhood.

"Darcy," I said, "you are starting a new, challenging phase of your life. School will be hard. You'll need real sleep and grown-up habits. You can't keep crashing on your own couch. You deserve a modern, adult-sized bed with a supportive mattress, and that doesn't mean you're letting go of your mom, just her bed."

It was hard, but Darcy did it, and it led to a cascade of changes that set her up to put her past behind her and rock grad school.

Whenever I see a messy, crowded master bedroom in an otherwise tidy family house, this tells me the lead parent is putting everyone else's needs ahead of their own. When it's a couple, there are intimacy issues. If the client lives alone, he or she is keeping secrets. Some of the biggest secrets clients have divulged—"I've never told my family I'm gay," "My children don't know I placed a baby for adoption as a teen," "My late husband had an affair"—have come out in the middle of a bedroom purge. My clients have literally tried to bury their secret under their bed or in the window seat or at the back of the dresser. If this is you, just ask yourself if your needs always come last or if there is something about yourself you are afraid to let people know. For every one of my clients, once they get that out in the open, their desire to smother that part of themselves below stuff disappears.

Master Closet

This is the room where we have to confront our physical selves every morning, and we can create a lot of chaos to avoid that. Lori had had gastric bypass surgery the year before and lost a hundred pounds, but she called me in because she had started substituting overbuying for overeating. She would justify it by

saying, "If I find something that fits with all this loose skin, I buy ten of it." But there was only one of her—and a seriously overcrowded closet.

Your closet should be a tool that helps you get out the door quickly, or it's time to look at your Clutter Blocks. Like Angela, are you buying clothes for a life you want but not the life you have? Or if your closet has become a museum of the life you led, the times you've had, you might be up against Clutter Block #1. People frequently freeze their look when they were their happiest.

I also never like to see a closet telling a client that they are X pounds away from happiness. There shouldn't be a rainbow of sizes or pieces unworn for years. Or fancy clothes going out of date and fading on the hangers. That tells us we've met Clutter Block #5.

Recently, one of my clients who is a mom felt like she desperately needed a makeover, even though she had no budget for it. Nevertheless, she got rid of all her worn, tired, stained athleisure clothes and started wearing her own "nice" clothes she'd been saving to wear since who knows when. She started promoting her old dating wardrobe to evenings out with friends. She shopped in her own closet and gave herself an upgrade in the process by deciding that even a trip to the supermarket deserved jeans and a real sweater.

Master Bath

A cluttered bathroom is what I call magical thinking central; it's where unrealistic expectations and Clutter Block #4 reign supreme. These are my makeup and product junkies who want to believe that the next lotion or the next potion will fix *everything*.

Recently, I was at a charity event with several former supermodels, women who had made fortunes on their looks thirty years ago. And how did they look now? Like women in their early fifties, because there is no magic solution. If there was one, these women would have found it.

It's painful to discover Clutter Block #7 and have this reckoning in the medicine cabinet, because we are not only looking at a lot of wasted money but also a fundamental lack of self-acceptance. Can you believe that you are perfect, just as you are?

If you have more than $200 of partly used products in your bathroom, please promise me you are going to start actively working on some serious self-love. No one will ever find you more beautiful than when you recognize it in yourself, so start there.

Kids Room

Every kid has clutter. Kids are clutter magnets, like Pig-Pen from *Peanuts*. In fact, my friend Nicole describes her daughter's room as where "hope goes to die." But if you can never see the floor, something deeper may be going on and asking you for attention.

When my clients' kids have been given too many toys, it's invariably about guilt over too much time at work or a sick grandparent or spouse. While it may seem harmless, there is a consequence to an overcrowded space—neuroscientists at the Princeton Neuroscience Institute found that excess stuff in your environment has a negative impact on your ability to focus and process information,* and the number one thing my clients who are parents are always trying to get their kids to do is focus and process information. The results of their study showed that clutter competes for attention, resulting in decreased performance and increased stress. That's the opposite of what parents are going for.

I deeply appreciate how hard it is to balance work and parenting; some of my clients struggling the hardest with toy overbuying are single moms. To move past this and make their kids' rooms a place they love to spend time, I encourage them to separate out the two issues. In their minds, the time issue can be solved by toy buying. But it's like solving stress with a cupcake. In the moment, you feel better, but the cupcakes will become their own problem.

---

* S. McMains and S. Kastner, "Interactions of Top-Down and Bottom-Up Mechanisms in Human Visual Cortex," *The Journal of Neuroscience* 31, no. 2 (January 12, 2011): 587–97.

Garage, Basement, Attic

Most Americans can't park in their garages because they have packed them with stuff they want to keep but can't deal with. A cluttered garage or attic tells me we are dealing with Clutter Block #3, or delayed decision-making that could be tied to Clutter Block #6. Clients have inherited a bunch of furniture they don't actually want but can't give themselves permission to part with, so they pile it in the attic or garage, hoping that someone will magically appear to make the decision for them. I've seen thousands of garages with mounds of furniture in the middle, like two dining room tables piled with boxes of late parents' objects. Invariably, these people are kicking the clutter can down the road because they don't trust their judgement.

These spaces are also where I see Clutter Blocks #4 and #7 in full force. "I've always wanted to take up rock climbing, so I bought all the equipment for it, but then it turned out I have vertigo." Block #4. "But I paid so much money for all this rock-climbing equipment, I can't possibly get rid of it. Maybe the vertigo will pass." Block #7. See how sometimes the blocks overlap to really keep us stuck?

I am going to tell you something: in Dante's *Inferno*, one of the most important pieces of Western literature, the lowest ring of hell is reserved not for murderers or thieves but for the indecisive. It was worse that these people had spent their lives making no decision at all rather than a poor one.

Ask yourself: What am I holding onto all this for? Can I trust myself to know what I really need?

I think you can.

Memorabilia

Be on the lookout for overcrowded or overabundant memorabilia as you do the tour. It can crop up in literally any room. I have clients whose bookshelves are crowded with Little League trophies from seasons long past. Trophy cases, glory walls, and commemoration of any kind that is over a decade out of date needs to be revisited and rethought so that, like Grace the ballerina, it isn't telling you that your best days are behind you.

In the Chinese school of home arranging, feng shui, they say leaving that stuff for so long causes stagnation. I love that word, primarily because it is kind of gross. I don't want my house to feel like standing water! I want movement and an opening to possibility, and that's where happiness and empowerment come together…in forward movement, not in being stuck in the past. So maybe just take it all down and redisplay everything, but shake it up. Or maybe take it all down and only put half (or a quarter) back up? Make space for something to surprise you.

Because at any age, life always can!

THE CLUTTER FREEDOM QUIZ

Grab a pen and let's walk around your house and answer yes or no. If you don't have any of these specific rooms (garage, home office, etc.) or don't have kids in the house, then skip those categories. But if you find yourself saying no to something but only because of a loophole (like keeping your electronics clutter in your kitchen), it's a yes. Total the number of yeses for each room.

GARAGE	YES	NO
Do you need to park your car elsewhere?	O	O
Is the middle of it filled with a collection of boxes that were from a previous move?	O	O
Is there stuff in the house that actually should be in the garage, like potting soil or tools, but it can't fit in the garage because you have equipment like bikes no one rides anymore?	O	O
Does walking into your garage fill you with dread and fear?	O	O
Is it full of belongings of people who have passed away?	O	O
TOTAL	☐	☐

ENTRYWAY	YES	NO
When you walk in the door, do you feel overwhelmed?	O	O
Has it become a place unfinished household projects live, like shopping returns?	O	O
Is your entryway missing a place for things you need to grab, like keys?	O	O
Is the hall closet full of jackets and shoes that haven't been worn in over a year?	O	O
Is there sports equipment remaining after	O	O
a household member giving up or outgrowing that sport?	O	O
TOTAL	☐	☐

LIVING ROOM	YES	NO
Do you have out-of-date electronics? A huge CD or DVD collection?	O	O
Are there piles of books on the floor?	O	O
Have children's toys taken over?	O	O
Do you wish you could redecorate but can't because of what you'd have to clear?	O	O
Do feel embarrassed at the thought of having guests in it?	O	O
TOTAL	☐	☐

DINING ROOM	YES	NO
Is it impossible or very difficult to eat at the table?	O	O
In the corners, do you have bags or boxes of items you don't know what to do with?	O	O
Are there seasonal decorations from the wrong season?	O	O
Is this where kid's art projects and old homework go to die?	O	O
Does the thought of hosting a holiday family dinner make you sick to your stomach?	O	O
TOTAL	☐	☐

KITCHEN	YES	NO
Do you have multiples of the same food product bought in different years?	O	O
Is the pantry spilling onto the countertops?	O	O
Are non-food-prep-related items living in the kitchen?	O	O
Do you feel completely stressed out when you try to prepare yourself a delicious and healthy meal?	O	O
Do you eat out or order in just so you don't have to spend too much time in the kitchen?	O	O
TOTAL	☐	☐

KIDS' ROOMS	YES	NO
Is the floor no longer visible?	O	O
Does it take longer than fifteen minutes to put everything away?	O	O
Does the top of the desk resemble a goody bag?	O	O
Does leaving the door open cause you anxiety?	O	O
Is the state of this room a constant cause of family fights?	O	O
TOTAL	☐	☐

MASTER BEDROOM	YES	NO
Is the top of the nightstand no longer visible?	O	O
Do you have boxes or stacks of paperwork lurking in the corners?	O	O
Do you have exercise equipment serving as a clothes rack or gathering dust?	O	O
Do you have to move clothes out of the way to get into bed? Do you sleep somewhere else?	O	O
Is the state of the room keeping you from getting a good night's sleep?	O	O
TOTAL	☐	☐

CLOTHES CLOSETS AND DRESSERS	YES	NO
Do you leave your clean clothes in the laundry basket so you don't have to fight putting them away?	O	O
Do you need to call in a search party to find a particular article of clothing?	O	O
Do the shoulders of jackets and blazers have dust on them?	O	O
Does trying to find the right outfit in the morning cause you to be late?	O	O
Have you cried more than once trying to get dressed?	O	O
TOTAL		

BATHROOM	YES	NO
Does the cabinet look like an aisle at Walgreens?	O	O
Do you have an abundance of unopened beauty or bath products?	O	O
Are you using the shower or bathtub for storage?		
Does the thought of taking a bath make you tense up instead of relax?	O	O
Does getting ready in the morning fill you with anxiety?	O	O
TOTAL		

Give yourself 10 points for each yes, then divide by the total number of rooms you scored. For example, if you answered yes to all five questions in all ten rooms, then your score would be 500/10 = 50.

1–15: You've got a good handle on your possessions, but the trick to staying ahead of it is tune-ups. Devote a few minutes each day to putting away, not putting down, and you'll stay clutter-free.

16–30: You have stepped into the danger zone. If you don't get a handle on your clutter soon, you will no longer own your stuff—your stuff will own you.

31–50: Don't panic; I'm here. Now is the time to really drill down and see what's under the clutter. Why can't you let go of stuff, and why do you keep bringing more stuff into your home?

Three Steps Back

The last thing I want to leave you with before we dive into the big purge in part 2 is that, in my experience, clutter starts three steps back. This means that whatever the sore area is for you in your home, your decluttering starting point is actually going to be somewhere else. Here is a story of my client Judy, which shows both that clutter is always asking for something and that it never starts where the problem is.

Judy, a mother of three teenagers and a full-time bookkeeper, hired me to help her reclaim her living/dining room so she could host Thanksgiving. I took one look at the piles of jackets and sports equipment on the table and asked, "Can I take a look in your entryway closet?"

She balked. "But I just need you to help me with the dining table!"

I asked her to humor me, and lo and behold, it was packed with boxes and paper shopping bags, preventing her kids from putting their gear away. She explained to me those were all items she took from her mom's house when she died—five *years* prior.

Judy's eyes watered, and her shoulders slumped. So here was the Emotional Clutter Block we needed to address. She was trapped with other people's stuff, Clutter Block #6.

"If you haven't had time to tackle this, why aren't these boxes and bags from your mom at least in the garage, out of the way?"

Yesterday

Today

Tomorrow

Because—bingo!—her garage was so packed full of old toys and equipment the kids had outgrown that she couldn't even park in it.

So we started prepping for Thanksgiving in the garage, where, it turned out, Judy was keeping all her kids' old childhood stuff for her someday, imaginary grandchildren. When I asked her why, she said, "Well, what if I die young like my mom? My grandchildren won't know me, but if they have the toys and clothes I bought their parents, they'll get a sense of who I was."

Once she said it aloud, she realized she was relinquishing her entire garage to prepare for something that, most likely, would never happen. Just because her mother had died when her children were little, there was no predictor that history would repeat itself. So we cleared out what the kids no longer used, getting ruthless about what really needed to be saved for the imaginary future grandkids, and made space for her mom's stuff, which emptied the closet, which cleared the dining table. After Thanksgiving, I returned, and we finally tackled her mom's stuff, getting the keepsakes down to a few things that went into the house to be used every day.

By getting at Judy's core issue—the loss of her mother in her past and the fears it had created for her own future—we were able to markedly improve her present. We gave her family their home back. Now she was able to have family dinners, not just at Thanksgiving but every night, and she felt like the last few years before her kids left for college were some of the best they had together.

So as I move you through this process, hold two things at the front of your mind. First, clutter starts three steps back, so the issue that's driving you crazy is not where you're going to need to start. And before we bag everything up, we're going to allow this crazy pile of stuff to reflect us back to ourselves, which may feel uncomfortable, but at every step of the way, I'll be telling you stories about my clients who found happiness waiting for them right on the other side.

They took the chaos in, heard what it was asking for, and embraced the changes, making space in their homes, hearts, and lives for the future they wanted.

PART TWO

getting down to it

4

before you begin:
set yourself up like a pro

IT WAS ONE OF THE MORE FRANTIC CALLS I'VE EVER GOTTEN.
A couple, David and Tom, had hired an organizer a few days prior. She
said she would get started setting them up while they were at work,
and then they'd be able to tackle the job over the weekend. It sounded
good, but when they came home, she had placed all their stuff from
their garage and basement on their front lawn and told them they
weren't allowed to go back inside until they had figured out what to
throw away. She literally barred the door. Panicked and embarrassed
as neighbors started staring, they jumped in a cab and went to a hotel,
where they stayed until their neighbors assured them the woman had
finally left. I now think of her as the Clutter Terrorizer.

Yes, there is a method for getting rid of excess and useless objects, but it has nothing to do with public shaming. I helped them get everything to their back patio, toss the stuff that was obviously trash, and then organize what remained into categories to make it easier to sort. By the following weekend, they had a garage ready for the upgrades they were planning and an organized basement to store what they decided to keep.

In this chapter, I am going to take you through all the nitty-gritty, step-by-step components for a successful purge. And do not worry—none of this is going to happen where your neighbors can watch.

Setting Expectations

So here we are, ready for the purge. You have taken a cursory inventory of your stuff and asked it what it might be trying to tell you about why you amassed it in the first place and what Clutter Blocks you might have. In this chapter, I'm going to take you through everything you need to do this as if I was right there beside you, making it all go smoothly.

The first thing we need to do is set your expectations. I'm not here to dispirit you, but I am here to tell you there is nothing magical about this process. People call me all the time because an article in some magazine or a book told them a certain project would be a simple afternoon's work, but it ends up overwhelming them. We are here to break the proverbial eggs on the way to a great omelet, so don't get dispirited if it gets worse before it gets better, or if you hit a Clutter Block and suddenly think, "I can't let go of this stained purse, cracked side table, or rusty can opener!" If you find yourself in conflict, remind yourself that clutter is emotional and that, in essence, no matter how aggravating you found your clutter, you are also stripping away layers of comfort or coping mechanisms that worked for you for a long time on some level. This process of getting conscious about your clutter habits is an investment, and like all investments, it means a little discomfort now for long-term joy later.

I will give you lots of tips and tricks for hanging in, but I want you to expect this to be hard. If it turns out to be easy, that's a bonus. But every week, I see houses with a few garbage bags in the corner from a project started and abandoned when the going got tough. I don't want you getting bogged down, feeling bad about yourself, and abandoning ship.

I believe in you, and I know you can finish this. I am right next to you, singing the theme from *Rocky*. Let's get going.

What Are We Going For?

What I stress to clients is that, rather than a showpiece, your home is your greatest tool. It has to work *for* you. It has to make your life easier and make you happy to be in it. What it doesn't need to be is color-coded, labeled, stacked, symmetrical, and monochrome.

Don't get me wrong. I love Pinterest, I love Instagram, and I love looking at perfectly organized spaces, but I rarely set my clients up in them. They're incredibly unrealistic. No one has the time to decant cereal into matching containers with chalkboard labels. No one has only one color in their closet. Life is messy. Life is chaotic. And all the manufacturers of groceries didn't get together and coordinate their labels to make your cabinets look pretty.

We are not going for Stepford wife. We are not going for laboratory experiment. And we are definitely not going for Instagram brag. I don't need you to put all your bathroom essentials away in pretty boxes if that makes them harder to get to! Obviously, if you want to, then knock yourself out! But what we are going for is a space that works efficiently for you and your family—one you can navigate easily and that looks beautiful to you. Beautiful because it represents overcoming emotional obstacles and attaining freedom. So we're going to set you up for success in your home, in your life, and no one else's.

Create Your Vision

This is not a woo-woo step; this is a very concrete and essential step that will get you through the challenging spots. With all my clients, I always ask what they want before we begin. It can range from feeling calm when they walk in the door, to having people over without feeling ashamed of their space, to simply knowing where their possessions are at any given time. Whether the goals are material or emotional, they are clear and urgent.

We will come back to yours whenever you hit a wall—which you will. You'll unearth some object or confront a Clutter Block that will stop you in your tracks for a moment or make you want to put this whole thing off another year. That is when you have to ask yourself: What is more import-ant, your goal or this item?

The answer will always be achieving your goal.

Take a Photo

Or twelve. Capture the chaos. It will feel so gratifying when you're done to have people over and show them what it looked like before. You can also share them with your friends on social media, but give yourself that opportunity for glory by taking some really honest pictures now.

Getting Ready

I know it may seem counterintuitive for me to send you shopping right now, but before we begin, you're going to need a few things on hand. Of course, I have to issue a standard warning here: if you are someone who tends to overpurchase, do not go overboard. You can always get more of any of this later if you run out. Before you head to shop, double-check that you don't already have all these.

I am also a huge fan of using your clutter to declutter. Do you have a bag of bags in the closet? Or boxes of boxes in the garage you've been squirreling away for just this reason? This is their lucky day! They are about to get called into action.

These are the tools I arrive with at every job, and they will be indispensable:

1. Trash bags. Only get them as big as you think you will be able to comfortably lift when they're full. So do not buy lawn and leaf or contractor size unless you are expecting some brawn to show up at the end and remove them.

2. Used boxes. Your local liquor or grocery store probably puts out dozens a night, or check the free stuff section on Craigslist where people who have just moved will list their used boxes. Stock up.

3. Hanging wardrobe boxes. But only if you are expecting to have a lot of clothes to donate that need to remain unrumpled, like business clothes for the charity Dress for Success. The caveat is that they are heavy when full, so only use them if you are planning on calling on professional muscle to get them out at the end. If not, then used shopping bags are your best bet.

4. Post-its in four colors. To label Keep, Donate, Recycle, Trash.

5. Sharpies.

6. Box cutters.

7. Packing tape.

8. Rubber or latex gloves.

9. Masks. The amount of dust hiding in very clean homes where stuff has amassed will amaze you. And with dust come dust mites, the invisible bugs that live on our dead skin and eventually take over pillows, headboards, mattresses, and couch cushions. Also, silverfish live in paper, corroding it, and mold can lurk in any damp spot. Save yourself the clutter cough and get some masks.

10. Dust rags.

11. Cleanser (optional). I tend to just wipe everything down with water, but if you prefer a stronger cleanser, get that too.

12. Stepladder.

13. Snacks. I am not kidding. You will get something called decision fatigue at some point, because the part of the brain that holds you to a task and helps you make decisions runs on glucose. When it runs low, you'll stop being able to think so clearly. I'll talk more about that later, but in the meantime, stock up on whatever you like to nibble on to keep going, whether it be fruit, nuts, potato chips, or Oreos—this is a judgment-free zone. I once arrived at a house-clearing job to find the daughter of the widower having a beer at 10:00 a.m. She was holding one of her late mother's sweaters. "It felt like this called for day drinking." No arguments. The only caveat: it has to be something that helps, not hinders the process. My day drinker went on to clean for the next eight hours after she finished her one beer. If it makes you need a nap, don't pick it.

14. Hydration. This is dusty work. This is manual work. Plan to drink water like you are working out.

15. Music. It can be a great motivational help but pay attention to it. One hour, you may need to be pumped up. Later in the day, you may need something soothing.

16. Kleenex. This can be an emotional process. Everything is here because you couldn't let go of it, but now the time has come to say goodbye. At some point during the purge, you may need to cry it out. Take your time and do not rush yourself through your feelings.

Researching and Planning Ahead

I know you're dying to dive in and go, but there are a few things you'll want to know ahead of time so that on the day, we don't have to stop cleaning and clearing to do research. You won't hold yourself up with procrastination that might actually be a Clutter Block masking as "due diligence." With the correct preparation, you'll know instantly if each item you *want* to get rid of *can* be gotten rid of, if it's recyclable, and who takes it.

Paperwork

1. First, call your accountant or tax preparer and ask how many years of back documents you really need to save. The rule of thumb from the IRS is seven years. After that, the statute of limitations expires.

2. Know that for business records, you don't need to keep received bills and invoices, just proof of payment, and most banks have

all your back statements digitally now anyway. This is my way of saying you can let go of most of what you've been hanging onto. If you have been avoiding dealing with this for a long time, face Clutter Block #3, and call your bank to find out how far back they keep statements. You'll be surprised how much you'll still have access to, and it will make letting go easier.

3. Schedule a mobile shredder to come to your house at the end of the day. They are very secure and time-efficient. You just bring your papers out to the truck. They put them in a large bin, and you watch as they are inserted and safely shredded. No worries about your Social Security number or other vital information being improperly disposed of, and no hours wasted sitting on the floor feeding sheet after sheet of paper into a shredder by hand, then unjamming it when it inevitably jams. Be sure to invite the neighbors. Make it a shred party! Every time we have the mobile shredder in front of a client's house, at least a neighbor or two will show up with a banker's box of paperwork and ask to join.

Recycling

1. E-waste. Do you have old phones, answering machines, TVs, appliances, batteries, wires, and cords? Get online and find out where your local e-waste recycling center is. Many Goodwill

locations also now accept e-waste. But know that does *not* include all personal grooming appliances. Also, if you are recycling a computer, smartphone, or tablet, do not forget to wipe its data first.

2. Plastic bags. Most drug store chains have a plastic bag recycling bin at their entrance. Don't put plastic bags in your home recycling bin, as they clog up the sorting machines at the recycling center. This is a great time to switch to reusable shopping bags, which eliminates the entire plastic bag issue.

3. Corks. Whole Foods now accepts them.

4. Fabric. Do you have lots of clothes that are clean but aren't in good enough shape to donate? Many cities now have fabric recycling organizations, and you should find out where your closest one is. You can donate clean clothes and textiles to be turned back into useful goods.

Donations

1. Know ahead of time who takes what. For example, it always takes people by surprise that they can't donate bed frames and mattresses. So before you think to yourself, "Oh, this'll all go to the thrift shop around the corner," call and make sure they take what you have. Some even take only seasonal donations.

2. Animal shelters are always happy to have donations of clean

blankets and towels. They may be too faded for you or for mattress sizes you haven't owned in years, but they will make some cat or dog a nice bed. Research shelters near you that accept donations.

3. Children in the foster care system are frequently moved with their possessions in garbage bags. If you think you're going to find suitcases, duffel bags, or backpacks in good shape, this is a great place to donate them. Find one near you.

4. Not all libraries take donations of all kinds of books. Check with them before you drive heavy boxes over. If they are at capacity, a nearby senior center might be grateful for paper-backs. Unfortunately, most of us know someone going through chemotherapy, so I often drop off lighthearted books when I accompany a friend for their treatment. Remember, if books are full of silverfish or are disintegrating, as painful as it is, put them in the trash.

5. In the United States, food expiration dates are pretty arbitrary. Every year, millions of tons of perfectly good food go to waste. If you're gearing up for a pantry purge and don't want the six cans of pumpkin pie filling you suspect are past their date, a food pantry nearby very well might. See which ones near you accept expired can goods.

Selling

1. If you think you have many items in your house you can sell, have a local auction house come over and give you an appraisal *before* you clean everything out. If it turns out they don't have the value you thought, you can include them in your donation, and you don't end up with stranded pieces you thought you could sell but are now just still crowding your home.

2. Many places in the country also have people who run estate sales right out of people's homes. This can be a great way to empty an inherited house quickly.

3. Do your research. Get on eBay, and don't go by the listing price. It doesn't matter if someone is listing the same cookie jar as yours for $1,000 if it doesn't sell. See if there is a market for your item. See if there is a glut of your item. See if your item sold and, if so, for what. Make an informed decision about whether it is worth your time and money to list your items or whether you'd be better off donating them—or throwing them out.

Disposal

1. Do you need to prebook a bulky item pickup with your trash company?

2. Doors must be taken off refrigerators, and you have to call ahead to have the Freon removed.

3. Mattresses must be wrapped in mattress bags. You can get them at the hardware store.

4. You may need to use a trash-hauling service if you have a dumpster's worth of stuff.

5. How are you going to get bags to the thrift shop, boxes to the e-waste facility, or antiques to the eBay drop-off? Do you need to schedule a man with a van? Does your husband or niece have a truck? Plan ahead so nothing gets stranded in your freshly cleaned home.

Plan Your Purge

I cannot tell you how many times I've heard, "I'm so excited. I've set aside the weekend to clear my house." While I applaud your enthusiasm, I want to encourage you to be realistic about your time and bandwidth.

In my experience, clearing, cleaning, and reorganizing a smaller area takes around four hours. So if you have a weekend to devote to this, plan four hours on Saturday and four hours on Sunday. If you want to do your garage, pantry, and closet, plan for twelve hours, ideally separated out over three days. Schedule it into your calendar like any other commitment. Pick a day far enough out that you can get all your supplies and all your research done, and then stick to that goal.

Additionally, this will take a lot of physical and mental energy. It's much better if you get to the end of four hours, ready to quit, and feel that you hit your mark, rather than feel like you're giving up halfway to an eight-hour goal.

If you have small children, plan to get them out of the house. In fact, if you have anyone at home who is going to be a distraction or who might pull you away from the task, plan to have them elsewhere. Mostly I'm talking about spouses or partners.

Once the area is cleared and cleaned and you have winnowed down what will live in that space, just putting everything away can take an hour. So plan backward from that. It might go faster, but I don't want you to plan to do all three in one day and then go to bed in a state of despair because you only did your pantry. If you go to bed on night one having rocked your pantry, I want you lying on that pillow with a big smile on your face.

Your Staging Area

Once you have all your gear, set up a good work surface. If you don't have a clear table or counter, borrow a card table from a friend. You'll want someplace you can separate things out from where they've been crammed, look at them one by one, and fold garments and bedding. Make sure it's an area you can dedicate to this for the whole process, which may last over several weeks. If you are going to do your attic, it could take a few four-hour sessions, so make sure your kids aren't going to come home at the end of the day and add their sports equipment or party goody bag to your staging area.

Your Plan of Attack

Plan your work, work your plan. Figure out where you're going to start. Remember, it is never where the most obvious problem is, because clutter starts three steps back. So begin by looking at the area that makes you crazy, like your kitchen counters. Is it the dumping ground for everyone's stuff, like backpacks and purses and homework? Why isn't that stuff able to go in closets? Are the closets packed with out-of-date and out-of-season items that should be stored in the garage? Then we're starting in the garage, clearing the too-small bikes and too-small clothes. Work backward to the source, and then go forward.

If the kitchen is on your list, I'd like you to make one breakfast and one of your standard weeknight dinners before you purge and keep track of how often you're crossing the room. Pay attention to the efficiency of your layout. This is especially true if you are trying to feed yourself—and others in your family—and maybe make a bunch of school lunches in the process. It's like a dance, and we want you to be taking as few steps as possible. Keep track, and the information you gather now will help when we put your newly pared down implements and tools away.

Planning for where these items are going to live after you purge will make it easier to decide if what you're keeping will fit in storage. For example, are you reclaiming the hall closet for towels and sheets? Then decide how many shelves will be sheets and how many shelves will be towels, and that will help you figure out how many of each you'll keep. This is a good place to remind you that if stuff is spilling out of closets and drawers, you have too much of it!

Unlike other declutterers, I don't have hard and fast rules about how much stuff people are allowed. If you have a family of six, you may need a ton of towels, but space is finite. If you are busting out all over, there are only two options: pare down your possessions or create more storage *in the home.*

For example, if your plan is to start in your daughter's room, take a glance before the purge and see what the biggest culprit is. If the room is drowning in books, you have three prep options: (1.) Do the work above to prepare to donate the ones she doesn't read anymore. (2.) Plan to clear more shelves for books. (3.) Before the day arrives, buy or make a new bookcase. But don't sit down to start going through all her books without already having set up some place she can put away the ones she wants to keep. You'll both get overwhelmed if items are moving from one pile on the floor to another pile.

That's why it's essential for a sense of accomplishment to get donations and garbage packed up and *out* every day. I cannot tell you how many homes I come to declutter only to find years-old bags of stuff from some previous purge still blocking the garage or entryway or dining room. Build the time at the end of the day into your plan, or hire someone to drive to the thrift shop, e-waste center, or dump, but know that whatever the area you're tackling first, stuff will be out of your home by nightfall. It will feel so good.

Also, plan to start with the stuff that is the least emotionally charged. Don't start with family photos, heirlooms, or the possessions of dead loved ones, because then your Clutter Blocks are most likely going to come up fast and furious. If you have Clutter Block #7 and feel the need to offset a financial mistake by ending your days still owning the pair of designer faux fur hot pants, don't start in your closet if that's where you made the bulk of your spending mistakes. Start with an area filled with items you can be objective about. So if you're tackling the attic, begin with the boxes of old commercial VHS tapes or the stuff a friend asked you to store "for a few months" ten years ago. Plan to leave the boxes you took from your mom's house six months ago until you have some road under your feet and you've built up some confidence in yourself from making lower-level, less threatening decisions.

With all this prep work under your belt, you are now fully set up for success and ready for the big day.

5

beyond the basics:
decluttering tricks of the trade

THINK ABOUT WALKING INTO A SPA FOR YOUR MASSAGE
appointment. The minute you walk through the door, you start to
relax. By the time you've made it to the quiet room, your shoulders
might have dropped an inch from your ears. Now think about when
you walk into your home. Do you feel the same sort of relaxation?
Humans aside, if your home doesn't make you feel calm, chances
are your clutter is to blame, and beyond the clutter, what's lurking
underneath it, whether it be shaky self-esteem bolstered through
shopping, grief that's never been allowed to be expressed, or a fear
of being wasteful that metastasized into a pathology. We've now
come to the excavation—both physical and emotional. Things may
get a little gnarly, but on the other side is freedom.

Guiding Principles

So you have assembled your supplies, forearmed yourself with your new Clutter Block awareness, and walked your clutter three steps back to find your start place. You are ready to go. Here are two guiding principles.

First, as questions come up—and despite the best planning they inevitably will—tackle them immediately. If you need to know if it's okay with your cousin if you get rid of Aunt Shirley's casserole dish, text her a photo *now*. If you need to know if it's collectable, get on eBay *now*. Today's mission is not to create tomorrow's to-do list.

Second, I am a big believer in pulling everything *out*, sorting it, and then only putting back what you want to keep. Yes, it's disruptive to empty the entire cabinet, closet, or shelf, but this goes back to selective inattention. We want you to see your possessions with fresh eyes and also shake your brain up a little to free your thinking. This is not only so you can look at the scarf your sister-in-law gave you ten years ago and you wore twice and say, "Someone else can enjoy this," but also so you can start to think, "Wait a second, the waffle iron doesn't need to be here! We haven't made waffles since the '90s!" Eurekas come on the other side of seeing differently. For that reason, we empty.

The Vision Steps

This process is about getting your stuff to meet your home in harmony. So before we pull everything out and examine the clutter, let's look at the rooms themselves. Here are five quick steps to set the intention for your purge:

1. Scan the room with your new perspective. What do you see?
2. Remember how it looked when you moved in. How did you imagine using this room then? Have you strayed from that?
3. What are three activities you want to be able to do easily in this room?
4. How are you taking care of yourself in this room?
5. What would it take for you to enjoy this room?

Once you have your answers, you'll be able to clear the clutter more effectively, because the items will either support your goals for the room or they won't. If that soccer ball doesn't fit with your vision, support three activities, or contribute to your self-care, it definitely doesn't belong in the master bath!

The Five Questions

The day has arrived! You have picked up your first item! And…you are stymied. I see this all the time, and it makes sense. You've lived with this carrot peeler, this pair of shoes, this receipt for so long. How do you know if you should keep it or let it go? Some of the stuff cluttering your life is going to stay, right? What if this bookend is one those?

I have developed five questions through which you can evaluate each item in a way that isn't leaning too heavily on the emotional connection, because when it comes to files, fishing gear, and toilet paper, we're talking about making your life work for you, and "sparking joy" doesn't really enter into it. If you want to keep it and you say yes to any of these questions, it can stay!

1. **Do you use it on a semiregular basis?**

   By semiregular, I mean at least once year, such as the large platter I have that holds the turkey at Thanksgiving. I have used it every year for over two decades, and it **stays**. The old sleeping bags that haven't been on a camping trip in ten years should **go**.

2. **Is it making you money?**

   Do you use it for work, or does it help you generate income somehow? It **stays**. Whatever is piled up in the corner of the family room for that someday garage sale that you're never going to have should **go**.

3. **Can you buy it again for a reasonable price or borrow it?**

   Is it costing you more to store it or fix it than it would to buy it again? Or is it something everyone has and it would be easy (and free) to borrow from someone you know? It should **go**.

4. **Do you have a place to put it away in your home?**

   Is it in a comfortable place where it fits easily? Great! It **stays**. Is it shoved on a closet shelf so that every time you open the closet door, it falls on your head? It **goes**.

5. **Do you love, love, love it?**

   I mean, do you *love* it? If yes, then it **stays**. If it's okay, I sort of like it, "I hate it but so-and-so gave it to me," it **goes**.

The Stuff That Is Going

Okay, so the item has met none of the five criteria, and it has to go. Now, how do you decide *how* it's leaving? Are you going to sell, donate, recycle, or throw away the item? If it's not obvious, let me help you decide.

Sell

Every day, a client with Clutter Block #7 says to me, "This is worth something." But is it really? And by that, I mean is there a resale value for it, and will someone hand you cash for this today?

Recently, I had a client send what she considered to be $100,000 worth of antique furniture to auction, and she only got $7,000 for them. She lost her mind, even though the auction company, her accountant, and I had predicted almost that exact amount. I'm here to tell you furniture is a diminishing asset. It's a tool for living, not an investment for the future. Sure, there are exceptions to the rule, but 99 percent of the time, furniture is to sit on, not send your kids to college with.

One of my clients, Elizabeth, had spent $1,500 on two antique Chinese chairs when chinoiserie was trendy in the aughts, but they were uncomfortable, and her new husband hated them. She wasted hours and hours getting them appraised and reappraised, finding dealers who dealt in Chinese antiques, and sending pictures of them around, with no takers. Weeks went by. They were in the way of her cleaning and clearing, and in the end, she donated them to Housing Works and got a tax deduction, which she wished she had done on day one.

If this isn't an item that you researched before you started, get online now and check the *sold* price, not the *listing* price. Ask yourself if that value is worth your time or if you are making more work for yourself that will bog you down from accomplishing your ultimate goal. What is your dollar bottom line, and are you willing to spend an hour on the internet to save ten cents on a can of beans? Imagine your time on one side of the scale and the satisfaction that money will bring you on the other. If you get serious jollies from saving ten cents, by all means, spend the hour. I personally think your time on this planet is worth more.

Donate

This sounds like a wonderful way to let items have a second life, but don't let this become an excuse to hold onto stuff. Don't give into Clutter Block #3 and say, "I'm going to donate this," as in, "someday." Box it or bag it up right now with a clear destination in mind, or else it goes in the dumpster.

Most importantly, is the item in mint condition? It's okay if you used something up or used it into an era when it has no value anymore. That is the nature of our fast-changing world. However, no one wants your broken, scuffed, stained, or nicked hand-me-down. Get very honest with yourself about whether the item has real reusable value to anyone right now, and don't be

upset if the answer is no. Time marches on, and no one wants a VCR or a cell phone the size of a toaster anymore.

Also consider the dignity of the people the organization serves. Just because they have a low income doesn't mean they want a ripped shirt or a stained pillow. I call this conscious donating. Be mindful of what your donation says about how you see the community you think you're benefitting.

Recycle

Hopefully in your prepurge homework, you already found out where a nearby recycle center is and what it takes. Bag and box it all up as you go. And again, make sure everything you're passing on is clean. If you recycle glass or plastic that's oily or greasy, the recycling center will have to toss it out.

Throw Out

It's okay. It happens. None of us want to be contributing to landfills, but that is no reason to let your home become one. I am giving you permission to throw some of your excess stuff in the garbage. Why? Because it is making you unhappy, and that is no good for anyone. When your house is clear and you are able to live the life you envision, that will be better for your family and your community. The garbage is the small price, and remember when you throw something away, where's away? Maybe this thought will keep you from buying disposable items in the future.

Like with Like by Function

As you go through your items, sorting "like with like" on purpose is critical. When your possessions are dispersed throughout your home, when there are batteries in the kitchen drawer and garage and hall closet or Advil in your medicine cabinet and kitchen and linen closet, you're dispersing your assets, and you're opening yourself up to repeat buying and waste.

But to do this sort, I don't need you to put your tea towels, your beach towels, your yoga towels, and your bath towels together and pare them down as one category, because that would be silly. Ditto with pillows. You don't have to play Sophie's choice with a throw pillow from the den and the lumbar pillow you sleep with. Each one performs a separate function, has a different purpose, and is stored in a different place. However, if you have thirty tea towels, including a dozen with the tags still on, none of which you want to part with, we need to look at what Clutter Block might be coming up.

When we're in the kitchen, we'll gather all the implements together from every drawer, crock, and shelf and go through them once, so you can see how many of each item you have. You might be storing knives or spatulas in multiple places and have way more than you need. Equally importantly, we'll stay on sorting implements until we're done with implements. If we jump to small appliances, that's called sequencing back and forth between categories, and that will give you decision fatigue much, much faster.

So now we'll go room by room and dig you out. Because of the three steps back principle, you may be starting in your master closet, and that's great! But I am going to go in the same order as our tour.

Entryway

Your entryway's job is to set you up for success for your day out or your evening in. So here is the rule of thumb for what stays and what goes: the entryway is the part of your home for items that leave your house, ideally on a frequent basis. These items include your keys, purse, shoes, coats, umbrellas, and possibly even luggage. If you have kids, their daily gear can live here too in a system we'll set up in part 3, but for right now, if items that live with you permanently have migrated here, it's time to escort them back where they belong.

Let's start by getting everything that doesn't belong out. That means all the errands to be run go in the car right now. If you can, enlist a family member or maybe even hire someone to run them. If not, your tomorrow just came into focus. You will run those errands and not let them clog up your hall another day.

If, like half my clients, your entryway is lined with UPS boxes, it's time to unpack Clutter Block #2 literally and figuratively. Figure out what you're keeping and what is getting returned, and then seal them back up and throw them in your car. Next time you're feeling a little lonely at night, think about all those boxes before you log on to Amazon!

Next, all the weekend sports equipment goes in the garage. If you only play tennis on Sunday afternoons or golf once a month, your clubs or balls and racquet bag don't need to be where you can trip on them.

Also, if your purse is out and your coats are piled on top of a chair, it tells me that this project goes hand in hand with purging the entryway closet.

Entryway Closet

Entryways get chaotic when there is nowhere to put anything away. Investing time and energy and maybe a little money in an entryway closet that works like a Swiss Army knife is worth it.

First, pull everything out of the closet. All of it. Entryway closets get very dusty, because they hold the items that go back and forth to the outside world, the dirt trackers, so once everything is out, this is a great time to vacuum the dust bunnies and wipe down all the shelves. If you're feeling truly ambitious, you may want to throw up a coat of fresh paint while you tackle the purge.

Let's start with outerwear. How many of those coats are outgrown or out of style? My Clutter Block #2 and #4 people may have dozens of coats with the tags still on. Every fall, from coast to coast, there are coat drives for the homeless. Someone needs that coat! As much as I encourage you to get everything out immediately, if you are doing this in summer, bag them up, label the outside of the bag "Coats for Donation," then place the bag in the garage prominently and put a note in your calendar for mid-November to drop the bag off.

Also, do you have to store all your outerwear in this closet, or could you swap seasonally? Hangers on any bar should be able to move an inch. If yours cannot, then the closet is overstuffed.

So often in client's coat closets, we find bags and bags of reusable market bags. Keep three or four good, sturdy ones, and use the rest for the donations you're about to make.

Have all your shoes migrated in here, making getting in the closet impossible? Here, keep the ones you either use frequently, like the pair you throw on to walk the dog or run the kids to the bus, or the ones you don't want trekking through the house, like rain and snow boots. The rest can be carried down the hall or upstairs to where you get dressed.

If have a shoe-free house, and the bulk of your everyday shoes are stored in the entryway, that's no excuse not to purge the shoes that aren't being worn or return the pairs that are worn only on special occasions back to your closet.

If you have kids' sports gear, check that the balls and bats and gloves are still in good working order, and make sure that everything that's sized still fits. This is the time to shout for family participation. Some cleats and gloves may need a quick try-on. Anything that doesn't fit gets donated to local youth organizations or posted on social media with the caption "whoever walks over first can have this barely used catcher's mitt! Hurry!" If your kids need to be able to dump certain objects, like bike helmets, and grab them again in the morning, separate them out, and we'll cover storage solutions in chapter 7.

Just so you know, items that don't belong here include: wrapping paper, framed artwork that hasn't been hung, old crutches, a lamp that needs to be rewired, and Christmas presents that were supposed to be given or returned years ago. Out, out, out!

Living Room

When I look into a client's living room, what I typically see is a repository of overflow from all the other rooms that are having their own clutter issues. Dry cleaning thrown over the back of the couch, along with laundry that was supposed to be folded and ironing that was supposed to be done at some point. Tons of toys. Boards on the floor still holding the round of a game abandoned weeks or months ago. Shoes. Tennis racquets. Pet food. I see it all. Do a quick scan and see what items can be returned to their proper place. Sometimes a quick removal of all the items that got dumped here instead of just being put away will declutter the living room in a very short time. But this is also where I hear a lot of, "I just don't know where to put these." If you pick up an object and don't know where to put it away, figure it out in under five minutes or out it goes. It does not get to spend the rest of its days on the back of your couch!

I know it's impossible to empty a living room the way you'd empty a closet, but if the shelves are cluttered, take everything off them and give them a good wipe down. Corral all the random stuff that doesn't have an obvious home into a pile so it stops looking like it belongs here. Sports equipment, toys, holiday decorations that never got put away—pull it all into one corner and then look back at how the room is supposed to look. Take a deep breath. Feels and looks good, right? That's your incentive for purging this pile.

And for the record, I am fine with having a children's area in your living room. It is your *family's* living room, for goodness' sake! If you are in there as a family, there should be something for everyone, and that may mean a baby changing station for a few months. You don't want to be running upstairs every time you need to change a diaper!

But there is a difference between a calm living room with a small table, an art cart in the corner, and bins of toys on the lowest shelf of the bookcase and a living room that looks like a day care center. If the baby is out of diapers, I better not see a box of them. It's not relaxing for you, and it's chaotic for them.

Even grown-ups outgrow stuff. So many of my clients have hundreds of CDs, cassettes, and even an eight-track tape or two thrown in but nothing to play them on. If you are storing a ton of VHSs or CDs, maybe hire someone to digitize all of it. Do you even need to own music at all, or can you get it all on Sonos, Spotify, or YouTube? Can you watch that movie on a streaming service? We should keep evolving, and our home should keep evolving with us.

Paper products are some of your living room's worst enemies, and magazines are the first item to make a room feel cluttered. Recycle anything you've already read or older than six months. If you have more than six months of back

issues of any one periodical you haven't gotten to yet, cancel the subscription. You may have aged out of interest in that magazine, which is fine! Save it for the hairdresser. Life is too short to feel the guilt.

For anything left before that six-month cutoff, be honest about the time and interest you have. Some of my clients with no time to read in their day-to-day life actually put their magazines in a tote so they're ready to roll for the next vacation or weekend away, but if you get on vacation and would rather nap, ditch them.

Finally, I can't tell you how many people keep other family's holiday cards indefinitely. These go en masse into recycling by Valentine's Day at the latest. You do not need to chronicle your dentist's family journey.

Dining Room

The way we live now, the concept of the formal dining room is falling away in favor of great rooms and multipurpose tables. Dining tables are also places to do homework, art, or office work, and I am delighted with all of that. I love a multifunctional space, but if you have a vision for the room that it currently can't support, like eating together as a family or hosting a holiday, then we need to purge.

I often call the dining table the road map to the other

problems. The items that have migrated here or started calling the table home are generally the ones that need to be put away elsewhere but can't be because the closet or drawer where they belong is overstuffed.

If I see a lot of paperwork, I know the home office area needs help. If I see a lot of sports equipment, it tells me kids' rooms or the garage need an overhaul. Folded laundry tells me we need to look at closets and bureaus. What are you seeing an excess of? What is that telling you?

Also, get really honest about your entertaining preferences. We are not the formal dinner party generation. If you're not using the china, donate it or—here's a crazy idea—use it! Dishwasher be damned. I hate to be the bearer of bad news, but there is very little china that has any resale value. And sadly, what you paid for it is no reflection of what it's currently worth. You know the factoid that the minute you drive a new car off the lot, it has already depreciated 25 percent. That's the reason Warren Buffett only buys used cars. The same holds true for your Lenox. China doesn't appreciate; it depreciates.

I inherited my grandmother's china and never used it. It had a gold rim, and I never wanted to take the time to hand wash it. But when my brother and his wife had to move to Los Angeles unexpectedly and had to quickly furnish a home, I realized it was time to rethink the china. So much better it was put to use than languishing in an upper cabinet! It gets run through the dishwasher every day, and yes, after a few years, some of the gold is fading, but it has been *used*, it has been *loved*, and it has served a *purpose*.

So maybe the extra china is going to be moved out of here and into the...

Kitchen

This is the room where you nourish and sustain and treat yourself; it's potentially the hub of your family (if you live with others). But it's also the container of tools. Only the garage can out-tool the kitchen. So this is where I see a lot of good intentions masking as clutter or vice versa.

Recently, when I wanted to make some badly needed space in a client's drawer, I pulled out a small clay bird and quizzically showed it to him. "Oh, that's super useful!" he said. "You put it in the top of a pie, and it lets the steam out."

Um, can't you make the same hole with a knife? Oh, and he made one pie a year.

We have all fallen prey to a cute gadget that promises the moon. But if you open the drawer and ten cute gadgets fall out and you've used none of them, we might be looking at Clutter Blocks

#2, #4, and #7. Do you drink tea? No? Then why do you have ten boxes? Do you really need a collection of tea balls when you don't drink tea?

Let's pare you down to the tools you rely on. As we go through the kitchen, I want you to ask yourself, what can do double or triple duty? Do you have an apple peeler and a vegetable peeler, a rice cooker and an Instant Pot?

Speaking of the Instant Pot, I also see a *ton* of unused wedding gifts. In the '70s, it was fondue pots; in the '80s, it was woks; in the '90s, people had to have their own ice cream maker; and in the aughts, it was bread. Now it's the one-pot meals and slow cookers. Be wary of the unitasker, the gadget or small appliance that only serves one function. Those things will create clutter in a hot minute.

The kitchen is really multiple areas with different purposes and issues, so we're going to break it down.

Countertop

- If it's cluttered, then everything is. Let's start here, because I want you to clear it all away, then only put back what is absolutely going to live out in plain view. Everything else has to get put away, which will force you to purge the cabinets and/or pantry.
- If there are two competing appliances, something has to give. I recently had a couple who each had their own coffee pod

machine, a Nespresso next to a Keurig. (Not to mention the drip for when their parents visited.) I said, "No. We are going to sit here and blind taste test until we find a coffee you *both* like, and then that's the machine you keep."

◆ Anything that doesn't support your vision for the kitchen or have a station gets cleared off the counters.

Lower Cabinets

◆ Pull out all the pots and pans and evaluate which ones are burnt, sad, or old. Are there duplicates from when you and your partner first moved in together? Or from recent inheritance? Has the nonstick surface gotten scratched on old pans? *Definitely* let it go. That %^&* is toxic.

◆ Anything that you don't use regularly can be donated to Goodwill if it's in good condition. If not, metal recycling.

◆ How many cutting boards do you really use? Can you keep the ones in good condition so that they double as serving platters for cheese and hors d'oeuvres?

◆ Same goes for cookie sheets, baking forms, and cake pans. Did you get all of this as wedding presents, but it turns out you don't actually bake? Or you used to do a ton when your kids were little, but it's been years since a bake sale? Let it go.

Drawers

◆ Empty every drawer and spread out all the utensils and serving ware. Melted spatulas can go. Duplicates can go. The egg spoon you've never used can go. Ditto dull cake servers and ugly cheese knives. Aunt Sally won't notice if you get rid of it, I promise.

◆ Let's take a look at your food storage. Do all the bottoms have tops, and if so, do they all still seal? Or have they been put through the microwave so many times that they're warped? Note that if the plastic has taken on pigment, it's no longer sterile. It's porous, which means it might be harboring bacteria, including listeria. Time to recycle and shift to glass! Also, takeout containers from restaurants are not made of a grade of plastic that is reusable over and over! Recycle them.

◆ Unless you are practicing for a circus act, you don't need more than ten knives. You just need one or two really great ones for large food prep and then a bunch of sharp paring knives. Many stores offer knife sharpening, which is cheaper and more environmentally friendly than buying another set when one gets dull.

◆ The takeout menus and manuals are all online. Recycle them, and just keep the manuals for the appliances *you still currently own and don't know how to use*. The blender? I'm fairly certain you know how to use it.

◆ I'm sure you have the all-American junk drawer. Empty it out fully, if only to give yourself the joy of finding something you lost and the horror of finding something you did *not* think you still had. Like an ex's car keys. In fact, pair every key you find with a lock, and if you can't, in metal recycling they go. Also, if this if your parents' home, keep your eyes peeled for keys to a safe-deposit box. I have found *dozens* over the years.

Upper Cabinets

- Most people need about half the coffee mugs they currently have. Get rid of the chipped ones, the ugly ones, the ones from the corporate retreat. Also, if your children have been painting mugs on the weekend, don't feel you have to keep every one. Hold onto your favorite and chuck the rest. Be ruthless.

- Are your dishes chipped, scratched, old, sad? Are you using something depressing while your "nice" dishes languish? That is Clutter Block #5. You are worth the good stuff! That is now your everyday, and the old stuff goes.

- How often do you run your dishwasher? If it's every other day, you need two water bottles and travel mugs per person. If it's every day, you only need one. Also, remember that the free ones leak, so the water bottles from camp or birthday parties should go straight in recycling. Buy everybody one good hot/cold bottle with their name on it, and you're done.

Pantry

- Contrary to what my grandmother believed, spices eventually lose their flavor. Ground spices maintain potency for three to four years and leafy spices one to two years. Here's a quick tip: write the month and the year the spice was purchased on the lid.

- We all have lots of food in our cupboards that our families won't ever eat. But at the same time, many people are going hungry. So when doing your pantry purge, call your local food bank and see if they take slightly expired food. Most do!

- This is also a great time to take stock of what foods really get eaten. If you went through a big couscous phase a few years ago and then burned out, donate it! Did you buy a ton of legumes with the plan of soaking and cooking them but never did, because you just don't have the time? Ditto.

- I like to make a master grocery list that lives on the computer and can be printed out. That way, before I go to the store, I can check the pantry to make sure I don't buy staples I already have. To stay ahead of the clutter in the pantry, never go to the store without a list. It's a surefire way to overbuy.

Family Bathroom

While this room might be a haven for miniature water sports, it doesn't have to feel chaotic.

Tub

♦ First, take everything out of the tub area and see if your kids still play with each item. Don't ask them, because they will say yes, even if they're on their way to college. Whatever isn't being played with anymore, pass along to friends with younger children, or put on a parent listserv in your area. The rest can easily get corralled into a mesh bag that suctions onto the wall. For younger kids, make a game of getting each piece out every night—and putting it away.

♦ Do you have half-empty bottles of shampoo and shower gel? Leave one in the tub and put the others in the medicine cabinet to be swapped in as the other finishes. Kids don't need too many options. Also, so many brands (even organic) make a hybrid bubble bath/shower gel/shampoo, so you can get it all done in one bottle if you wanted to combine them.

Medicine Cabinet

♦ Do you have outdated medicine? Baby thermometers but no babies? Tiny Band-Aids but no tiny toes? Anything unopened and unexpired can be donated to a women's shelter.

◆ Have your older kids grown out of playing with the temporary tattoos/jewelry/nail polish/hair chalk? Pass it along to a friend with younger kids and make their next rainy day.

Kids' Rooms

Even for the best-intentioned parents, this can be where hope goes to die. I promise you, the fewer objects your kids have to keep track of, the better job they'll do keeping their rooms clean. Unlike adult purges, kids' rooms have to be done regularly. I recommend using the change of the seasons as a trigger.

Closet

◆ When there's a been a growth spurt or it's gotten warmer or colder and everything needs to be tried on, purge everything they've outgrown and clothes they've been given that they're never going to wear, like that dress from Grandma your tomboy wouldn't be caught dead in or anything too scratchy or itchy. Everything in great condition can be passed along to friends or shelters, and anything stained but clean can go to fabric recycling.

◆ Take your kids' words for it. If they say, "I'm never going to wear that," believe them and pass it along.

◆ When considering clothing saved for imaginary future

grandchildren, pick one or two garments per year *tops* that are worthy of being passed down. The hand-embroidered, the smocked, and the enchanting go in a clear, clearly labeled storage bin with a tight lid called the "grandma box." The rest gets passed along *now* to children living *now* who need clothes *now*.

A word about buying kids clothes: I cannot tell you how often I help a mom get rid of bags and bags of clothes that still have the tags on that she bought on sale, guessing at what size her kid would be a year or two out. Nine times out of ten, they guessed wrong, and the corduroy pants that were 30 percent off at Crewcuts got skipped over when they jumped a size. It's not a bargain if it never gets used. It's much better to buy clothes for opinionated kids that reflect what they want *now* and fit them *now*.

Toys

+ I urge my clients to use a one-to-one ratio: for every gift received, something must be donated. An upcoming birthday or a visit from the grandparents who come with suitcases full of toys is the perfect time for a proactive purge.

+ I recommend involving the kids as much as possible so they learn how to let go and you can start modeling for them that you value a clutter-free space as a family. For five-year-olds and up, I like to put a big bin in the middle of the room and let them have first crack at filling it with what they think they can let go of. Then we go in and do a second round. "Do you *really* still play with this [headless] doll? *Really*?" That can usually shake loose another whole garbage bag. Lastly, there's the "wait until they're at school to take out the toys you know they haven't touched in months or years" approach. Also very efficient.

Art and Paper

- I am giving you permission to throw out your child's artwork. Please don't let their childhood become Clutter Block #1. You need to save one turkey hand picture, not three dozen. Pick one or two pieces from each year, and save them nicely in an acid-free box, because if you don't curate, you will be drowning in construction paper. You can also take a picture of their work and then have a photo book made. As far as art walls, kids want their most recent accomplishments reflected back to them. Don't put up everything from preschool and then stop. Keep rotating in their new work and putting the old stuff in the trash or storage. Also, keep going back and looking at the trove with fresh eyes. The piece of paper with cotton balls glued to it that made your heart swell five year go may now just be garbage.

* Do not save daily homework assignments. Save the special ones, the essays, the funny stories, but one or two per year. They'll be all the more special because they won't be buried under a hundred pages of the multiplication tables.

Master Bedroom

In my twenties, I had a friend who had a reasonably neat bedroom. All that was in it was her unmade bed and a large pile of clothes. One evening while she was showering (she was always running late for our plans), I decided to hang up some of the clothes in the pile. Her closet was actually empty, so over the course of the next half hour, I paired the bare hangers with the balled-up clothes, and I discovered two amazing things. One, she actually had a really nice slipper chair under all those clothes! I had never known that. And two, on that chair was a bag of what had once been apples and was now a bag of green fur.

The master bedroom and bathroom should be an oasis. It's where you start and end your day, but too frequently, I'm called in because the bedroom has become a dumping ground. If you're picking your way to your bed through piles of magazines or a maze of old exercise equipment or the bones of a home-based business, you won't feel serene before bed or supported when you wake. Nothing gets the day off to a bad start like waking to a pile of clutter. I empower you to take your suite back.

Nightstands

- How many of those books stacked up there are you actually going to read? Pick *one*.
- I recently had a client who had *three* iPads on her side and *three* on his side! Recycle them to Apple, and you'll get a gift card!
- Now clean out the drawers of empty foil pill jackets, old chocolate wrappers, Kleenex, and hearing aid batteries. Nightstand drawers are garbage magnets, and that's not what you want by your head while you sleep.

Furniture

- I encourage all my clients to take a scan of how many of their possessions are pieces they chose and how many are inherited. If they inherited the furniture, I encourage them to reexamine if it's really functional. Frequently, the answer is that if they had a *four*-drawer dresser instead of the *three*-drawer dresser they inherited, they could actually get that pile of T-shirts off the top.

+ Are all the glides in working order? Are the drawer pulls intact? Is the cover on the slipper chair clean and appetizing? If not, the furniture is going too.

+ I am all for storing out-of-season clothes under the bed in zippered bags or rolling trays, but if you have a ton of stuff you don't want to deal with stashed under your bed, like old paperwork or a late relative's clothes, that stuff must go.

General Clutter

Clutter in this room is like drunks in a bar at closing: I don't care where you're going, but you can't stay here. When I hear, "I don't know what to do with this," I know people really mean, "I don't actually want to own this." All too often, this is the room where anything my clients can't decide on gets dumped. Unfinished projects, undonated items, unreturned clothes. None of it belongs here, and I am giving you permission to let it go.

+ Do you actually want all your late mother's costume jewelry? If not, pass it along to cousins, or donate it to a local theatre.

+ If you have a framing project, go to your calendar right now, and block out your next available time to take your measurements and drop it off or mail it away if you're using a company like Framebridge.

+ If you haven't finished your wedding album, enlist your crafty cousin who loves to scrapbook. Or there may be someone who has started a business doing this in your area. Google it.

* If you watch TV in here, have you also amassed a VHS player, DVD player, and dozens of outdated remotes? Get rid of all dead electronics.

* If old dog or cat beds are beyond being refreshed by a run in the machine, it's time for new ones.

* Yes, it's a cliché, but every week, I see an elliptical being used as a clothes rack. If you are not using your exercise equipment several times a week, out it goes.

* If I see clothes everywhere, that tells me the closet is overstuffed or you've fallen out of the habit of putting things away. It stops today.

Master Closet

It's a fact that we wear 20 percent of our clothes 80 percent of the time. We *all* have too many clothes, and I'm as vulnerable to the siren song of another blue blouse to go in my blue blouse collection as the next girl. So I get it. I really do. But your closet is a tool, and if it's too crammed for you to get dressed easily, then it needs a scouring. Just remember, as with the entryway closet, hangers should be able to move one inch side to side, and there should be one inch at the top of any pile before the next shelf. If there is no daylight anywhere, let's do this:

✦ First, let's get real about what you actually wear. Are you saving clothes that aren't your current size? If it's too big, don't leave it in your closet for "when you get fat again," and if it's too small, don't keep it to beat yourself up about your current size. Your closet should be full of the clothes you wear and feel good in *right now*. Not the somedays or the I used tos.

✦ Are you saving clothes for when your kids grow up? Are they *really* going to want them?

✦ What's the state of your jewelry box or drawer? Don't forget jewelry periodically needs to be purged too! Pass along the costume stuff you don't wear to your kid's costume box or a local nonprofit theater.

✦ Do you have boxes and boxes of memorabilia on the floor or the top shelf? Do you need to put on some Depeche Mode, open a bottle of Whispering Angel, and cull it down to one shoebox? We all had a prom. You probably don't still need the commemorative champagne flute, and it for sure doesn't need to live in your closet. Now is the time to eighty-six it.

✦ This is a great time to invite a stylish friend over. Bribe her with a spa date, and then try on everything while she reads magazines on your bed and tells you what to keep and what has had its time and place.

Master Bathroom

This room should be your retreat. It's a place to practice self-care, and if it feels cluttered and cloying, it's a missed opportunity. Clutter Blocks #4 and #7 frequently partner here. If there are lots of barely used products for your fantasy life, this is definitely where it can feel wasteful to throw them out. But if your bathroom is bringing up feelings of remorse or if you look in your medicine cabinet every day for the product to "fix" you instead of take care of you, then your refuge becomes an emotional land mine. I want to free you from that. Return to your bridge and mantra as you clear out the excess.

Medicine Cabinet

- This is the place to get honest about all the beauty products you don't use. I know they were expensive. I know they promised the world, but if you didn't like the way they smelled or felt on your face the first time you used them, you're never going to. Offer them to a friend. Bring a bag of purged beauty products to your next BFF lunch, and watch the products get snatched up.
- Makeup has an expiration date, collects bacteria, and can give you pimples or pinkeye if used beyond that date. The closer to the eye, the faster it goes bad.
- Purge sample sizes. If this isn't in your color or skin type, pass it on!

- If you subscribe to a service that sends you random makeup and beauty products every month, consider canceling that subscription. It is basically a clutter-delivered-to-your-door service.
- No one uses those tiny hotel bottles when they get home. If you have dozens of them, remember, runaway shelters and homeless shelters *need* toiletries. Don't hold on to something you don't need that someone else can benefit from.

Drawers

- Old hair bands, hairbrushes, and toothbrushes can go.
- As can curling irons and straightening irons if your hair hasn't been long in years.
- Old toiletry bags with expired products—out, out, out!

Under the Sink

- This is the place for a couple of rolls of toilet paper, a hair dryer *maybe*, and a couple of cleaning supplies. If it is crammed full of other things, they don't belong here.

Tub Surround

- Think about products that can do double duty. Shave gels and foams are actually just conditioner. They soften the hair to make it easier to shave. If you already have conditioner in your shower, that's one less product cluttering the scene.

♦ What do you actually use daily? Pare down the products around the tub to the essentials. Your shower should not look like the sale bin at CVS.

Home Office

This is a place where you want to be able to take care of your life's business quickly and efficiently. If you have Clutter Block #3 and you're swimming upstream against the room before you've accomplished anything, your life is going to get more and more stressful.

♦ The number one cause of paper clutter is overretention. Everything you identified in your prep that's superfluous can go.

♦ Regarding receipts, which are their own mountain, only keep the ones that prove what you've bought *if* it applies to a business deduction. You don't need to keep the receipt for that pack of gum you bought at CVS in 2015. I promise.

Photos (From Every Room)

This is a *gigantic* project. I never recommend doing photos during a decluttering purge, because it will get overwhelming, and the rest of your goals won't get met. Here are some tips for doing it *after* you have the rest of your house exactly how you want it:

- Lots of people suggest scanning all your old photos. It's an option but a very time-consuming one. If you are going to digitize your old photos, then do a pass and purge the bad photos, the duplicates, the closed eyes, the pictures of people whose names you can't even remember. If you aren't a talented photographer, throw away all photos of places you visited with no people you know in them. That's what Google images is for. Then organize them chronologically, if even by decade. If you don't organize before you digitize, you'll just have the same mess on your hard drive.

- Get them all into one physical place. Meaning take the ones at the top of the closet, the ones in the garage, and the old albums in the den, and put them on your staging area table and go through them in one slog. This way, you'll know what the crème de la crème is, and it will be easier to get rid of anything mediocre.

- I have a client who threw away all the pictures her parents took while on cruises in the 1990s. She said, "I have no idea who any of these other couples were, and none of these pictures have anything to do with how I remember my parents." How do you remember and tell your family history? Does this tell your family history? If not, it goes.

◆ If you don't want to put them in albums, just get acid-free boxes, organized by decade.

A last word on photos. When my grandmother died, one of the items I managed to take from her place was a giant box of black-and-white photos. I was waiting for a "good time" to sit down with my dad and have him tell me who everyone was. Well, I lugged this giant box through two moves and was about to move it a third time and thought, "Wait, this is ridiculous." Next time my dad came to visit, we sat down and went through them. He was sitting at my coffee table and looking and looking and getting more and more confused and befuddled, until finally he said, "Tracy, this isn't our family."

It turned out my grandmother had been storing boxes for a long-deceased neighbor, and now I had been carrying around *her* ancestral photos for the better part of a decade.

One great picture, printed and out where you can see it, is worth a thousand in a box.

Garage

I cannot tell you how many clients have crammed their garages full of filing cabinets, old toys, old clothes, and inherited items they don't really want. They park their cars in the street or in their driveway and live next to a teeny, tiny enclosed landfill. This is *not* a storage locker. This is not where you get to shove everything you can't deal with. This is where you keep your car, your gardening equipment, your laundry tools if the machines are in here, and some bins of seasonal items. That's it. Filing cabinets? Out. Old toys? Out. Anything you use so little that your solution was "Just shove it in the garage"? Out, out, out!

A word about bulk shopping: only buy in bulk what you use in bulk. If your kids have moved out, it might now take you a year to use thirty-six jumbo rolls of paper towel. I see so many garages packed with multiples of items that seemed like bargains but are now just taking up space, creating clutter and stressing out my clients. Think carefully before you put the item in your cart. A bargain isn't a bargain if it comes at the cost of your calm.

Attics and Cellars

First off, the general rule is that with the exception of holiday decorations, if you didn't need the item enough to put it where you can grab it easily, let it go. If you don't camp, if you haven't rewired the lamp, if you have boxes you never unpacked from the *last* move, if you haven't used the punch bowl, the artichoke plates, the trundle bed, or the Pack' n Play, donate it. Or you may need to get a hauling company.

Yes, I am advocating for an empty attic and/or cellar. You are probably storing way more than you need, and your house will breathe easier when it's lighter. I want to throw out a radical concept: just because you have storage space does not mean you have to fill it. Contrary to popular belief, it is okay to have an empty basement, an empty attic, a garage with only a car and automotive accessories in it. Not every cabinet and crawl space must be crammed. We have a compulsion to store items like squirrels for a *someday* or a *maybe* or a *down the road.*

Today is the day to ask yourself, can I pass along whatever it is that is living in a box somewhere in my home that is tricky to get to?

Depending on your age, you may want to put an ad up at your supermarket and have someone bring everything down or everything up for you. If you are going in the cellar, wear a mask, as the damp can be bad for all sorts of breathing issues.

Storage

Are you spending money for off-site storage, and do you know how much you're spending? Because every time I ask a client how much they pay for storage, they underestimate the answer. Like cable companies, storage facilities give low rates to lure new tenants and then gradually raise them annually. Go look right now at what you're paying. You probably have it set to autopay on a credit card and have no idea what the actual annual cost of your excess stuff is.

Here is God's truth about storage. With *rare* exceptions, you don't need anything you have in storage. How do I know that? Because it's not in your house! It's not where you can grab it and use it! If you have to get in your car and comb through boxes to find the whisk, it's not a whisk you need.

I am laying down a challenge: whatever month you are reading this book, dare yourself to empty your storage facility by the end of the calendar year. Once you've tallied what you're paying in storage, decide that you are going to use that money next year on a vacation. Maybe it will just be a local spa weekend; maybe it'll be a flight to Europe. Or put it in a high-yield savings account. Even stuffing it in your mattress is better than paying for storage. I cannot stress this enough—do not fork over money every month to store what you don't use and are avoiding making decisions about. The cost is too high.

6

when the going gets tough: breaks, breath, gratitude, and friends

AT SOME POINT IN THIS PROCESS, YOU WILL MOST LIKELY hit a wall. Some unearthed object will provoke your Clutter Block and unleash a flood of emotion, and it will feel too painful to proceed. Or the sheer volume of what you have ahead will make you want to walk away entirely. We once pulled back a bed and found a mummified cat behind the headboard. We take breaks too.

When my client Betsy's husband died, she was devastated. Her kids had helped her clear out the house and office a bit, but no one wanted to touch the garage. Not because it was so scary but because it was *full* of hundreds and hundreds of boxes containing Ron's impeccably catalogued library of rare films and TV shows, mostly on VHS tapes. He had taped them off the TV and then organized them by genre, director, star, etc. There were also hundreds of commercial tapes on a variety of formats, all with memories and history. Betsy was now in Clutter Block #6, trapped with Ron's hobby, which was disintegrating in the garage. She was coping with it by convincing herself that something he had invested so much time and passion in must be worth something to someone.

"Someone will want these," she said. "I'll pay to send them to veterans' homes."

I told her even veterans' homes have DVD players now.

The realization paralyzed her. She was near tears, so I suggested a walk to get a coffee. We walked in the sunshine, got a delicious iced coffee, and treated ourselves to a vanilla scone. Recognize when you might need to walk away for a few minutes and replenish that valuable brain glucose!

"You know," she finally said, "if the garage was empty, I could move everything else out of storage and save money every month." It was a great idea, so the hundreds of tapes went to e-waste. A few months later, she called to tell me that with the money they saved, they had a silent movie restored in his honor, which was such a beautiful tribute. Much better than a garage full of disintegrating old tapes.

So rest assured, almost everyone hits one of these moments along the way. It is *not* a stop sign, but it does require taking a moment to call in some reinforcement. In this chapter, I trouble-shoot the most common crises and help you move through them to attain your goal of a clutter-free home that supports your best life.

Snacks and Breaks

As I mentioned in our shopping list and as Betsy so perfectly exemplified, studies have shown that we need glucose to replenish the part of the brain that makes decisions. The kind of purge you are undertaking is going to cause something called decision fatigue. That means, at some point, you will pick up the next object and genuinely be unable to make a decision about it.

Stop. Put it down. You literally, cognitively cannot go any further. This is where the snacks I asked you to buy come in. Go eat something. Take a walk around the block. Watch a quick funny video on YouTube. Stretch! Give yourself a ten- to fifteen-minute break and allow your brain to regroup.

This also might be a good moment to switch to a smaller project. If downsizing the Christmas decorations feels too emotional, stop and go do the spice cupboard. Come back to the Christmas decorations when you're rested.

To that end, plan your day so that you are tackling big or emotional projects in the morning when you're fresh and small projects, like the linen cupboard, at the end of the day when you're fried. Or plan to purge all morning and drive around dropping donations off all afternoon.

But bookmark your breaks, and by that, I mean set a timer. Don't let five minutes turn into three episodes of *Grey's Anatomy*.

Don't pick snacks that will make you sleepy. My drug of choice is an iced coffee with cream for fat and a little sugar for glucose. That can keep me going through anything.

Gratitude

I know gratitude might seem like a strange emotion to bring in here in the midst of one of the hardest projects you've tackled in your life, but it can be really helpful. First, it shifts your brain out of being overwhelmed. So pick one thing in the midst of the chaos to say you're thankful for, even if it's just finding my book!

Gratitude also replenishes willpower and helps you take back a sense of control. Ultimately, you *chose* all this stuff, and you *chose* to leave it where it was. I'm not saying that to be judgy but rather liberating. You can make different choices! That is a place of power. Be grateful for that.

Also, it doesn't make you *un*grateful to get rid of excess possessions. If you didn't grow up with a lot of material possessions, it might feel spoiled or thankless to be throwing things away. It's not. It's a gift you are giving yourself to bring what you have and where you live into balance. Be grateful for the awareness of wanting that harmony.

If you are looking at twelve scarves from your mother but you don't wear scarves, fill yourself up with gratitude for her love, pick one to always remind you of that feeling, and pass the rest along.

You have enough. You have more than enough. You can take a big sigh of contentment around that. Now we're just paring you down to set you up for success.

Support

People call me in because this is hard work to do alone. So ask a friend to give you a hand and be that emotional support you will need along the way. But it has to be someone who is going to encourage you to let go. If your best friend is also struggling with excess or disorganized possessions, they are not the person to help (unless you're going to take turns doing each other's houses, which I think is a wonderful idea).

If you don't want anyone physically there with you, send out an email a few days before you start to your best friends.

Hey, guys. I am about to undertake this big project and am anticipating that it might get overwhelming at times. Expect that I may call you for a pep talk at some point. Thank you for your love and support.

This way, you don't have to start the SOS call by catching them up on what you're doing. You can cut straight to "I just found my Dad's cuff links. Help!"

But I also want to caution against thinking you need someone to come to your rescue. Many of my clients waited for a family member to come help or a weekend everyone could pitch in, and that weekend never came, and the problem just got worse. Don't give your power away by thinking you need someone else to show up and get this done.

Just because you can't deal with everything doesn't mean you should do nothing. Pick one area, no matter how small. Clean it, clear it, put what you're keeping away, step back, and admire your accomplishment. This is what success feels like.

What to Expect in Process

As some areas come into balance, the areas remaining might feel less and less comfortable. Don't let that discourage you or freak you out. It means the clutter no longer has a hold on you.

You may also have to do some parts in rounds. Maybe you begin with the garage, but then you do a really deep purge in the kitchen, and that feels so good, you realize you left a lot of things in the garage that you could really part with. That doesn't mean you failed at the garage. That means releasing your Clutter Block is gradually shifting how you see your home. I love when this happens for my clients.

Revisit Your Vision

If a snack, a break, and a pep talk from a friend didn't get you going again, it's time to revisit your vision. Are you fighting credit card debt from your overbuying, and is your vision living debt-free? Are you and your family members fighting all the time, and do you need to reclaim a room of your house for serenity?

Say it out loud.

"This feels hard right now. I'm exhausted and overwhelmed, but I want to eat at my dining table next Sunday, and I am going to, and it's going to feel amazing."

Hold to that vision.

Is This an Emotional Clutter Block?

Have you run up against one of the seven Emotional Clutter Blocks? What was your bridge? It's time now to dive into it in more depth and set up long-term action plan. That might mean finding a therapist. That might mean calling a debt consolidator. That might mean notifying your family that you are getting rid of Grandma Rose's bedroom set and anyone who wants it has thirty days to make arrangements to pick it up. Whatever reinforcements you need to call in to be able to release this excess stuff, now is the time. You deserve to get clear of this Clutter Block. Your bridge is now your guide.

What is on the other side of that bridge? Living in a place where you have released the need for the clutter so that it never, ever comes back.

Financial Reckoning

All of us have a moment where we are confronted with the cost of our clutter. This could mean adding up storage fees you've been turning a blind eye to or simply adding up what you've spent on items you've never used. Sitting with this is an important part of the process.

I had a client, Ted, who asked me to clear out a storage facility his wife had kept in Malibu for over twenty years. When I got in there, all I found was a bedroom set. When I asked her about it, she said, "Well, I was saving it because if my son and daughter-in-law ever move to California, they might want it."

"A thirty-years-out-of-date bedroom set?" I countered.

"Yes," she said.

"That's a lot of ifs that need to line up for that set to be used again."

She wasn't fazed. "It stays."

"Can I just ask, how much is the storage?"

"It's nothing."

I took a deep breath and went to find someone who could help put a more concrete number on "nothing." I looked over the paperwork and saw that when she first signed her contract, she'd been paying twenty bucks a month, but with annual increases, they were paying close to $400. I opened my calculator app and tallied.

"Elizabeth," I said gently, "you've spent $32,000 storing that bedroom set that cost—what—$2,000?"

She was floored—and mortified. Somehow in her mind, she was being frugal by keeping the bed. The *cost* of being frugal had never hit her.

Almost every client at some point has a gut punch of how much money they've wasted. Even me. Don't let it trip you into a new shame spiral, but sit with it.

And let it stop here. Contact your financial adviser. Make a budget. I have a great book in the resources section that can help anyone get their money back under their control. Don't let your stuff take from you anymore.

Heartbreak

Sometimes, something you've literally buried comes to the surface. I see it all the time. Two of my clients, a Korean-American couple in their late sixties, had literally put up a wall between them in their home. Their stuff prevented them from sharing a room, sharing meals, or even sitting together. As I was helping the wife clean out her bedroom, we found an old black-and-white Polaroid under the bed of a gorgeous Caucasian guy leaning against a convertible. She started to cry.

"He was the man I wanted to marry, but my parents wouldn't let me. They made me marry this man." By realizing that she was using stuff to smother her wound and literally bury her choices, she was able to clear out her home—and leave her marriage.

So if you find something that's heartbreaking, sit right down and let yourself be sad. Allow the pain to surface…or the grief. If at all possible, call a friend or family member. There's a story you need to tell. This is what was under your clutter. Let it have its say.

Shame

At least once a week, someone turns to me with tears in their eyes and asks, "How did I let it get here? Am I a crazy person?"

No, you are not. You most likely had one of the seven Clutter

Blocks, and you used clutter to create an emotional distraction from something that wasn't working in another area of your life.

Let's look at the successes in your life. I want you to list five things that you are great at right now. It could be professional or personal. Maybe you're a fantastic chef, a great manager at work, or an asset in your community.

Remember, not everybody is good at everything. For example, yes, I can declutter, but I struggle with delegating and saying no, and my karaoke game is awful. I also just realized that in an attempt not to be wasteful, I am kind of hoarding disposable plastic to-go cups instead of bringing a reusable cup to the coffee shop. It's a process for all of us.

The important thing is not to let this go into a shame spiral. As Brené Brown defines it, the distinction is that guilt is "I did a bad thing," and shame is "I am bad." Shame leads to clutter and hoarding. We do not want you turning this purge into a cycle for more stuff to roll in.

You are a normal person who simply let one area of your life get away from you. What systems do you need to put in place moving forward so this never happens again?

That's what we're going to focus on in part 3.

PART THREE

arriving and thriving

7

strategies and systems
to organize what's left

THIS IS THE FUN CHAPTER! YOU HAVE BROKEN THROUGH
your Clutter Block(s), and here is where we look at what you kept,
room by room, and figure out how to put it all back to ensure the
greatest ease of living. I want your home to be a sanctuary that
makes you happy every time you return. I want you to be able
to get you and your family out the door with minimal effort and
have your evenings feel restorative.

This doesn't necessarily mean minimalism. If a bed covered
in throw pillows makes your heart sing, I am all in favor! If you
are a family of five or six, you might have a lot of stuff. But what
fits comfortably? I want you to focus on the number of shirts,

tablecloths, can openers, and pogo sticks that can genuinely fit in your closets, drawers, and cupboards so that you can see everything and nothing is crammed in. If, when you go to put things away, you are still having to lean your body weight against the closet door to get it to latch, pull everything out and get ruthless.

In this chapter, we're going to go room by room as I make suggestions, based on my years of experience, for how to organize your possessions. There will also be lots of handy illustrations so you can see what I'm talking about. Also, check my Instagram feed (@tracy_mccubbin) for great before-and-after images to get you inspired.

Then in the second part of this chapter, we'll talk systems and practices. Ensuring that your newly clear, clean home stays that way, and it permanently relies on a two-pronged approach. The first you already did by getting at the emotional roots of your excess and taking action. The second is about putting practices in place to make sure that you stay on track. Think of it like getting sober from clutter. Yes, the first huge step to a clutter-free home is making the change, but the work is committing to clutter sobriety over the long term.

Also, if you find that you want to go back to buying for someday or not opening your mail or letting relatives store their possessions under your roof, revisit your bridge. Remind yourself that you have a proclivity and a vulnerability to one or more of these Clutter Blocks. Don't get down on yourself, but look at it through that lens and be vigilant. When addicts are getting sober, they avoid bars. Maybe you need to create some really strong rules around acquiring, but we'll talk more about that in chapter 8.

Now, I want your home to work for you, and I want you to live the life you always pictured in that home. This is how we'll make sure that happens.

Putting Away

This is a part of the process that always freaks my clients out a little, because they don't trust themselves anymore. How do they know that where and how they want to put something away is right? I frequently see that they've let that fear and distrust of themselves prevent them from taking any action.

As I've said, making decisions fatigues your brain and is one of the reasons people who live in visually crowded homes find being in them so tiring. Every time they need something, they have to rummage to locate it, and every time they want to put something down, they need to make a decision about where. None of it is automatic, so it's all draining their brainpower!

Don't let this happen to you!

Systems

One of the first things a new client will say to me is, "I just need systems!" People often think that we declutterers have the lock on some special insider technique that magically makes homes effortlessly spotless forever. But here is the huge pro tip: the best system that will keep your house tidy is simply picking a place for the items and then *returning* them promptly when you're done using them. There's no right or wrong to where that place is. Just make a decision.

But there is a caveat here. When I say place, I mean a spot that you can describe to someone over the phone looking for that item in your house. For example, "It's in the third drawer down under the microwave." I don't mean waving your arm at a pile and saying "Oh, it's over there," or "I know where everything is" when gesturing to a mountain of stuff. I meet those people every week who refer to their homes as "organized chaos," and they are kidding themselves. They do not actually know where their laptop case, carrot peeler, or house keys are.

Once your house is clutter-free, *you* decide where the kept item lives permanently, and then all you have to do is return it daily to that spot. That's it.

Your toilet paper can live on a caddy on your head for all I care, as long as you put it there all the time. When you find a roll on the bookshelf, it goes right back on your head.

You need to keep your makeup in the mudroom because that's where you have five minutes before carpool? Fine. One of my clients keeps her blow dryer in the drawer with her umbrellas—weird, right? Well, that dresser is right across from her daughter's bathroom, and it's the fastest place to grab it after bath time. It works for her. Again, none of this has to look like a catalogue or a magazine spread. Real organization for real lives. What I care about is that when your throat hurts and you want to make tea with honey, you know exactly where your tea bags are and can grab the honey as the water boils.

The habit to cultivate is not putting things down but putting them away, right when they come off your body, out of the dishwasher, or out of the grocery bag.

Visual Order

The key criterion to help you decide what goes where is how often is it used? If it's something you use daily, it goes at eye level or as close as possible. Eye level is prime real estate. The less frequently it's used, the farther up or down it goes. This is as true in your closet as it is in the pantry.

People process the world differently, and what's effective in one person's brain gives someone else anxiety. Some of my clients like to color code. Personally, I am pro labeling, as they serve as a reminder that you had a plan and a vision and as a road map for the rest of the family if you live with others. I also use my labels as a guide for the person who comes to clean and for my overnight guests. However, use your power with caution! Label the shelf where the twin sheets go "twin sheets" so the queen-sized don't migrate there, but if it's a cup of pens, don't label it "pens." You'll just invite everyone to tease you for stating the obvious.

Time Management

To make decluttering more enticing, I am going to throw out a really basic suggestion: podcasts and audiobooks. For thirty minutes a couple of times a week, combine something that *entertains* you with the super basic maintenance we all used to be able to find more time for.

Teamwork

If you live with other people who tend to make choices that run counter to your vision of a clutter-free home, this is the time to have a household meeting and set some rules. "This is what lives in here from now on, and this is what doesn't. Homework must be tidied off the table before dinner." Or, "Board games must be put away." Or, "Your dirty sports clothes go in the hamper, not on the floor by the fireplace."

Creating Order Room by Room

Entryway

Let the form follow the function. Is your entryway a workspace or a reception space? Many people have a formal entrance they never use and then something between the garage and the kitchen that does the heavy lifting. Whichever you traffic most, the following rules still apply. Who knows? You may like your new entryway so much that you start using your front door.

Regardless, is your entryway set up now to help you grab-and-go at the beginning of the day and easily unload at the end? If you pass your entryway into your home, and you're still lugging a bunch of stuff, that stuff is going to migrate to places it doesn't belong.

My entryway is a two-foot-by-two-foot area around my front door, what I call a landing strip: that place you can put things down so they don't end up on the back of the couch or the dining room table. There's a coat rack so my jacket and purse can come right off, a pretty bowl where my keys live, and a spot for my shoes. Do you need to put hooks on the walls? Do you need a long table for the mail and dish for your keys so you can walk farther into the house unencumbered?

If you have children, you might want a boot bench or cubbies. I frequently set clients up with a series of complimentary baskets of different sizes. One holds recycling, so all catalogues and junk mail are dumped right at the door, and the second holds soccer balls and the like. The third holds projects until errand day.

If you're a shoe-free house, get shelves or a big basket that can live in the closet or by the door. IKEA makes great ones that are slim and hide the shoes from view, and don't forget to declutter this shoe repository every few months.

If your entryway includes a staircase, you could utilize a basket for the bottom or the top, so that items that need to go up or down have a place to rest until your next trip.

If you have Clutter Block #3, let your new entryway help you. Open your mail right when you come in the door. Keep a recycling bin for catalogues and a shredder in a handy place near where you open the mail so it all gets instantly divided into three categories: recycle, shred, and actionable.

Do not even get me started on keys! They live in one of two places: on a key chain attached to your purse or backpack, or in a dish by the door. You do not ever come farther into your home than your front hall with your keys.

The front hall closet might also be a place where it's worth investing in some good storage solutions. Don't settle for one overstuffed bar and then a floor crammed with a jumble of stuff. There are lots of companies that offer prefab closet shelving that can be customized for your space at a reasonable price. I see so much wasted closet space. The floor is frequently underutilized. Do you have room for shoe shelves or bins on the floor? Then there is typically a lot of dead space above head height. What about luggage storage? Some people are even able to get a second hanging rack in. Now that you've purged everything that doesn't belong here, give what you kept room to breathe.

Houzz, Pinterest, and Google Images can be your friends. See what other people have done for their storage solutions. Because I promise you, if you have a problem, someone else has solved it.

Dining Room

Just as in every room, this goes back to your vision for how you want to use your home to live your life. If it's a priority to have regular meals at this table, let's establish some clear boundaries around it. This is the family meeting spot, not a sports rack, and feel empowered to lay it out for everyone you live with. "This is where we gather to eat and connect. Please put your socks elsewhere."

We touched on this in the purging section, but if this room serves multiple purposes, make sure each one is supported. If it's a homework or art place, get an art cart or a cart to hold laptops, pens, paper, and homework gear. IKEA makes a great one, or store art supplies in the sideboard now that you've passed along all that unused china.

If you're using the room for a home-based business, commit

and put some filing cabinets in the corner that you can drape with a matching tablecloth when you have people over and transform into an instant sideboard.

Perhaps you actually need some more furniture in this room, like a sideboard or a china hutch to hold holiday decorations and tableware. Antique ones can be had for next to nothing at most thrift shops these days. If the ornate look is not your thing, think HGTV and spray paint it a fabulous, unexpected color. You've instantly made something dowdy chic and given yourself somewhere to put away all your entertaining staples.

I recently moved clients of mine into their new house, and they 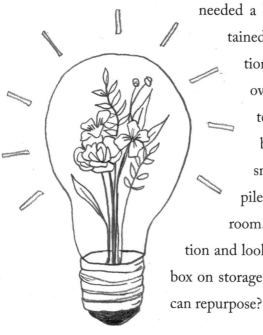 needed a bar area because they entertained a lot, but after the renovation, they had no money left over. However, their daughter had outgrown her ladder bookshelf in her room, so I snagged it from the donation pile and installed it in the dining room. It holds their tequila collection and looks great! So think outside the box on storage. Is there something that you can repurpose?

Living Room

How you want to use this room will dictate the way we set it up to work for you. Are your kids older and you'd like to reclaim this as a formal space? Or is it a family room? Overall, our culture is moving away from formal living rooms toward "great rooms," open spaces that are kitchen, dining, and living room all in one.

If your home has an open floor plan, for it not to feel chaotic, it's important that items stay in their area. The kitchen utensils stay by the appliances, and the place mats stay near the dining table. The ant farms and lacrosse sticks and the latest Costco run stay out of the picture altogether.

To make that work, I am huge fan of storage in plain sight. Fabric boxes on low shelves of the bookcase can hold kids' toys or the Wii accessories. An ottoman can hold board games or blankets for snuggling. A coffee table with drawers can hold coasters and napkins and remotes.

Of course, all these tips work for a traditional layout as well. Always look for items that can do double duty as places to put things *away*.

Kitchen

As you find a home for everything in this room, I want you to think command station and nourishment. If this is where your kids drop permission slips, maybe get an in/out box at the office supply store. If this is where you pay bills, get a box to keep them in all month long so you don't have to hunt through other papers looking for them at the end of the month. For a lot of my moms, we will set up a hair station in the kitchen, maybe just a little bucket with brushes, rubber bands, and clips, because while the kids are eating breakfast, Mom can get in there and whip out a fast braid. We've also added a sunscreen bucket. Don't put it tidily away in the medicine cabinet if that means the kids will leave without any on. Keep it on the counter, and apply it while they're eating their cereal.

If you're looking to be eating in a way that sustains and energizes you, clear the clutter so that meal prep is pleasurable and easy. By knowing exactly where your tools are, making dinner can become meditative instead of the fifty-yard dash.

Go back to the exploratory meals I asked you to make in the prep section. Was the cereal in one cupboard, but the raisins lived across the room? Was the coffee near the stove but the tea in the pantry? Do you need a coffee station? Do you want to have your fruit in a bowl on the counter so you remember to grab a few pieces before you head out? I want you to think about how you use the room and how you can set yourself up to be making as few trips across it in meal prep as possible. Because if you have to cross the room with the raisins, the chances of them getting put back drops. That means spices near the stove. That means all your breakfast items on the same shelf so you can grab them all easily and put them back quickly. Above all, it means you're not leaving a trail of items behind you.

I would also strongly recommend that you optimize your kitchen. My number one optimization tip (which also goes for bookshelves and medicines chests) is to *adjust* adjustable shelves. They were not assigned that height by the government, and they do not need to be at a uniform height from cupboard to cupboard unless you are expecting a poltergeist to throw all the cupboards open at once. Make sure each shelf is just a little bit higher than whatever goes on the one below, and you might be able to add one to two extra shelves per cupboard—that's gold! If you're staring at a lot of air, you can probably add a shelf.

Additionally, adding layers in your drawers or cupboards eliminates space around your cutlery or your spices. Dead space in the corner is the perfect place for a wraparound unit.

IKEA, the Container Store, and Amazon sell lots of options for organizing and maximizing, like vertical lid racks, cookie sheet holders, and steps to keep pots from getting lost in the back. But do *not* buy anything without measuring shelves, drawers, and cupboards first. (Even if you have an IKEA kitchen, not every IKEA accessory works for every drawer.) Wherever you are going shopping, measure every dimension before you shop, because there is nothing more annoying than getting back home with all your new gear, excited to get to work, only to find none of it fits.

Countertops call for a balance between serenity and practicality. I use an old cake plate of my grandmother's to hold my salt, pepper, and olive oil. It would be silly to store them away in a cupboard, because I grab for them two or three times a day, but they don't migrate all over the kitchen; they live on that plate.

Remember, the guiding principle is efficiency, not the photo op. It's about real organization for real people. It's about a springboard into your best day. Carrie Bradshaw kept sweaters in her oven.

You don't cook? By all means, use the storage.

Look, everything is a trade-off. For me, having clear surfaces makes me calm, so since I'm five foot three, using a ladder is part of my life. I'd rather have more stuff put away and clear counters and leave my ladder out where I can grab it.

Garage

Think about making the most of the perimeter but not the center of the room. Remember, the center is for your cars. Take a look at all the walls to see if they have storage potential. Scan your eyes up, and then scan down. Do you need shelving, a tool station, or a laundry station? It's fine for the room to do multiple duties, but set it up to do them well and still leave room for your car.

Also, please don't buy 120-gallon size bins, because when they're full, you can't lift them. Clearly label whatever you do bin or box away in the garage so you never have to rummage. Think of sending someone to your house to grab something. Could you say, "The nutcracker is in the garage in the third bin under the tool table marked Holiday House Decor"?

Little Kids' Rooms and Playrooms

Kids *love* to feel proud of themselves. So now that you have done your child the greatest service, which is paring their possessions down to what they actually use, you're going to do what I call setting them up for success. Give them storage solutions they can use, such as lightweight bins, and place books on low shelves so they can put favorite reads back in themselves. Recently, I had a mom who had bought these hanging mesh toy containers. She was so proud of herself, but they were too high off the ground for her three-year-old to use easily. She ended up having to bend down and clean up everything herself.

Think light and easy to maneuver for a small person. Most toy boxes are horrible; they have heavy lids, and they smash little fingers, but also think about where you want the items they can't reach, like the messy glitter or the fragile porcelain coin bank from Grandma.

In their closet, do you have the right hangers? Buy small ones, ideally with felt grip so that they can get the hang of hanging up their own clothes without it looking like a comedy routine. Are the closet rods low enough for them to reach? Here's another example of where adjusting an adjustable item will directly result in better organization.

Teens' and Tweens' Rooms

Their bedrooms now are less about toys and more about a functional space to think and work. Homework will be easier with a filing system and bulletin board to keep track of their own projects and work flow. Do they have after-school activities that need bins to keep them organized? Ballet gear can go in one bin, tae kwon do in another.

In general, kids this age like to have a *lot* of visual information in their environment. Posters layered over bumper stickers layered over concert tees stuck to the wall with more bumper stickers.

I support all of that! I just encourage parents to stick to a clean floor maxim. The walls can look like Instagram threw up on them, but they better be able to walk from the door to the bed without stepping on anything.

Master Bedroom

First off, making your bed is a sign of taking care of yourself and respecting your home. Give the you who will be coming home twelve hours from now the gift of a made bed.

Once you've purged the clutter, to keep the room feeling restful, what you do store here has to be put away cleverly. Take advantage of under-bed storage for extra linens. Get dressers that hold your clothes comfortably or an extra free-standing wardrobe. How about your nightstands? Do they have shelves for books or drawers for meds, ear plugs, or lavender foot lotion?

Beyond that, try to leave the rest of the room clear and clutter-free. This is where you unwind at the end of the day, and you don't want to be tripping over stacks of unread newspapers as you climb into bed.

Master Closet

Closet organization is one of my favorite projects, because they can look so beautiful afterward. And I love getting emails from clients saying, "I got dressed in five minutes this morning!" Your closet is a tool, so make sure you can see everything, because what you can't see, you won't wear. Clothes should not be crammed and shoved in your closet; if that's still the case, then it's time to purge again.

My rule is that chaos cannot reign in the closet. The guiding principle of closet organization is like with like: shirts with shirts, pants with pants, dresses with dresses. And above all, a closet needs to be color coordinated. That is how we pick clothes in the morning. If you've put on red pants and you want to find the camel-color sweater that matches, you should be able to glance at the shelf that has your earth tones and grab it.

This means that if you are someone who wears pants most days, they will hang in the most accessible spot, and they will transition from light to dark by season. So in the summer, you might have dark jeans transitioning to light jeans and floral fabrics, and then in the winter, you may swap that out for thicker jeans and dark wool to light wool pants. Hanging next to them would be your skirts, once again starting with the darkest and transitioning to the lightest or brightest color. Each garment category—shirts, blouses, sweaters—is also organized by color. If you live in a cold climate and wear primarily sweaters, they may get several shelves. Each pile should be its own sub category, based on what you reach for— V-necks, cardigans, turtlenecks, patterns. One of my clients lives in

wool turtlenecks. She has three shelves of them, and each pile is a different color family.

Obviously, not everyone has every color, but in general, use the rainbow as a guide. Black and gray together in one pile, then blues, purples, and greens in the next pile, then orange, reds, pinks, and peaches, and lastly yellow and white. That will look pleasing to the eye and make it easy to spot the item you're looking for. Keep in mind that most people tend to only buy clothes in three or four colors based on what flatters their skin tone. I rarely see an actual rainbow in anyone's closet. As a blond, my closet leans heavily on blues to match my eyes. Whatever your categorization, just keep them separated for easy mornings.

As far as what gets to go where, let's make sure your favorites are easily accessible. If you wear a dress to work every day, put those in front in order from casual to dressy—or the reverse. This way, even if blindfolded, you'd know that your work dresses are in front and evening is in the back. Then skirts, then pants, moving away from the door, if you don't grab those so often. However, if you wear pants every day, do it in the reverse.

Next, think weather. In the summer, the shelves at eye level might hold tank tops. But in the winter, move the tank tops to the top shelf out of sight, and put your wool go-tos at eye level. Swapping out your clothes twice a year forces you to keep seeing them.

Remember selective inattention? Do you not even notice all the cocktail dresses from your dating days that you wouldn't be caught dead in now? If they survived the first purge, now might be a time to be more critical. Edit ruthlessly.

When tackling your accessories, it's important to have the right tools. The Container Store has tons of options for storing and displaying jewelry. A corkboard with ribbon pinned to it can work great for hanging earrings or necklaces. Do you wear a scarf every day? Put up hooks for them where you can grab them.

Also, as you put away, you may find that one thing might tip it all into not working—the cowboy hat from that dude ranch visit or the crinoline from your wedding dress. It's time to get rid of that item.

In my experience, every room has a thing that is standing between clutter and calm. If yours is still here, this is your chance to let it go.

Bathroom

This might seem obvious, but do you have shelves in your shower? Even ones that suction to the wall if you can't drill will add a lot of order.

Baskets under your sink can help you organize the toilet paper* and the hair dryer and the heating pad so you never have to dig when you need them.

As far as creating visual order, matching towels and bathroom accessories are instantly calming. If you share your bathroom with kids, it's vital that their toys can be bagged up or put away for your wind-down time. No one unwinds in a day care. Don't get ready for bed in one.

Linen Closet

First, I am assuming you have purged all the old, ratty mismatched sheets and towels. Now, how to sort what's left? If you have a family with multiple sizes of bedding, label the shelves so anyone doing the laundry will know where things go back. Lots of people fold sets together, meaning fitted sheet inside flat sheet with pillowcases

---

* When it's not living in the caddy on the top of your head.

tucked inside. That way, when it's time to make the bed, you are only grabbing a complete set and not hunting for pillowcases. In my house, I use all white sheets, so I don't have to put any effort into thinking about what goes with what. It was a huge change for me. This way, if a bottom sheet gets stained or ripped, I'm not wasting the rest of a perfectly good set.

Most people have way more bath towels than they need. Assign a shelf and only keep as many towels as comfortably fit there. Beach and pool towels get their own shelf. They serve a different function and get stored separately.

The linen closet can also be a place for bathroom overstock. Use bins or shoeboxes to keep anything you buy in bulk organized, like dental floss, soap, and bandages. On a high shelf, you may want to store organized photos or Christmas ornaments or memorabilia.

Plan on It

Schedule a consistent window once a week to catch up with your home, and mark it in your calendar, like you would an exercise class. Ideally, this would be a time when you're not tired and you don't have a lot of people tugging on your attention. Some of my clients like to get up before their families on Monday mornings and put everything back in order for the week while the house is quiet. Me,

I prefer Sunday evenings, so I can wake up ready to go on Monday morning. By scheduling it, it will eventually become a habit, and you'll feel weird if you *don't* do it.

Markers to Keep You on Track

Weeks on from your purge, are you still able to maintain your goal? Are you still eating at the table? Are you getting out the door on time? Parking in your garage? If anything has gotten in the way of maintaining your goal, schedule a four-hour tune-up for yourself ASAP.

Three is the magic number. When you have amassed three of any item that doesn't belong where it's hanging out, it's time to address it. Do you have more than three days of unopened mail? Sit down and open it. Is your laundry basket full of clean clothes, but there are three new loads to do? Put the last load away. Do you have more than three things on the dining room table that don't belong there? A sweater, a library book, mail?

Hit three, time to spree. Which is my little saying, meaning if you've gotten to three, it's time to clean.

Maintenance

Maintenance is a wonderful opportunity to check in with yourself. Start thinking of your home as a barometer of how you are doing in all areas of your life. If your kitchen starts to get cluttered again, are you cheating on some nutrition promises you made yourself? If blankets are migrating to the TV couch, are you avoiding your bed for a reason? Continue to let your clutter talk to you and tell you what you may be emotionally avoiding.

Do you leave the house a mess at the start of the week because you get the Sunday blues? For those clients, I recommend forcing themselves to put on their favorite music at 8:00 p.m. and straighten up for thirty minutes. For my clients who find that they are tempted to cocoon in clutter in winter, I prescribe an annual sun break—or even a sun lamp! Are the holidays hard because your family is far away or you've lost someone? Don't let clutter become the comforting go-to. Instead, take action steps outside of your possessions to make yourself sustainably happier.

For the nitty-gritty maintenance, I use the seasons. I am a huge fan of spring and fall cleaning to set yourself up for a stress-free summer or an easy holiday season. Tax time is great for purging paperwork.

Take advantage of end-of-season check-ins. Don't just put away all the holiday decorations; get rid of the broken ones and the items you haven't put out for three years. Don't just put away the beach towels for next year; donate the ones that have gotten stained or shredded to an animal shelter.

Above all, think of these as tune-ups, not as signs you're slipping. You haven't failed. Your car isn't broken; it has to be taken in for regular maintenance to function optimally. A little clutter is just a sign that your home is asking for attention, for a tune-up.

Giving your home thirty minutes once a week will allow your home to give that time back to you tenfold. Every minute of your life you spend looking for things you own is a minute wasted. Even five minutes a day hunting for your keys adds up to thirty hours a year! Almost an entire workweek just hunting for your keys! Try to think of this maintenance not as a chore but as an act of self-care. Love your home, and it will love you back.

8

conscious consumption: how to halt the clutter creep

Now, after all your hard work, the fact is that I am sending you back out into a world that will push stuff on you at every turn. Every shop window entices; our inboxes are full of sale emails, promotional offers, and coupons; and circulars arrive daily in the mail. Every day, we are asked to buy, buy, buy.

Please know I am not immune to the siren call of a good sale or a little late-night internet shopping after a rough day. As a result, I have developed some tricks and tools over the years that my clients and I rely on to keep our homes pared down and functional.

How to Tell If This Might Be a Challenge

Certainly, many of my clients don't shop. They have been living under the weight of Clutter Block #6, Trapped with Other People's Stuff. Now that they have relinquished the items they inherited or were storing for friends and family, they are confident they will easily be able to maintain what I call eye peace: everything in their sight line will be soothing.

However, for my clients who have Clutter Blocks #2 or #4, where I walked in the house the first day and the entryway was lined with (or blocked by) Amazon, Rue La La, Gilt, 6pm, and Overstock boxes, I know someone has been numbing their feelings through shopping and that there are smothered emotions that need to be explored and given space.

Doing the work in part 2 and clearing out the old is similar to a twenty-eight-day detox for addiction. No one walks out of rehab thinking, "Well, I'm cured." It's really only the beginning of tackling the problem sustainably if shopping is a coping mechanism for you. How can you tell if shopping might be an addiction? Could you give up shopping for nonessentials for thirty days? If the very idea of that brings up a lot of fear or anxiety, your shopping habits are worth giving a closer look.

Why did the sales of lipstick soar in 2009 after the financial crisis?* We like to buy ourselves things to cheer us up, and all we could afford was lipstick. However, if you feel the need to spend money after you've finally cleared your clutter, ask yourself what emotional need shopping fills for you and if you can fill it in other ways. Perhaps pick up some flowers instead, or meet a friend for a walk. If you have items that are still in their bags or boxes, it's not about the stuff; it's about the feeling you're chasing.

Again, no beating yourself up. I'm just trying to bring gentle awareness so you are in a strong place to make different choices moving forward. The past has lessons, and if you learn from those lessons, there is value in those mistakes.

Perhaps you need a new practice in your life. Many of my clients have benefited from adding meditation, yoga, and even therapy into their arsenal. Ask yourself, how can I get that kick somewhere else that's genuinely productive? Because the thing about shopping is it *feels* productive, right? You *feel* like you're solving a problem. You found the shoes for the wedding, you can replace the worn-out bedspread—ooh look, they now make nonstick oven mitts! It *feels* like this is all about solutions.

Really, it is a problem. Each thing you buy and bring home becomes a problem. Something you have to store, wash, vacuum,

---

* Ekaterina Netchaeva and McKenzie Rees, "Strategically Stunning: The Professional Motivations behind the Lipstick Effect," *Psychological Science* 27, no. 8 (June 2016): 1157–1168.

dust, put away, dry-clean, repair, and hang up. It is on your to-do list in one way or another, and you don't need another thing on your list. I want you to start thinking of your life right now, with whatever you own at this moment, as perfect. You do not need one more thing to be happier, better, thinner, hotter, more desirable, more successful, or even better organized.

In fact, the next time you have the impulse to buy something, I want you to whisper, "I'm perfect. Just as I am. With what I have."

So let's pretend you are standing in a store. You are holding a new pair of shoes. Before you put down your credit card I'd like you to play through the following:

1. **Cost**

   This isn't about a random line item on your credit card statement, but what will these shoes actually *cost* you? What do you make an hour? If you don't bill hourly, take your weekly take-home and divide the total by the number of hours you work. That is the value of an hour of your time. How many hours will you have to work for those shoes? Two? Three? Ten? Are these shoes worth ten hours of your time? If you only have a finite number of hours to earn money in this lifetime, are these shoes something you want to trade those hours in for?

2. Debt

How quickly or slowly are you paying off your credit card? If you have debt with interest, those shoes might end up costing you far more than the number on the tag. According to a report by the Consumer Financial Protection Bureau released in December of 2017, the average American household with credit card debt is carrying a $15,000 balance. With the average APR of 16 percent, the highest it's been since before the financial crisis, those shoes could cost you double the sticker value if you take a long time to pay them off.

No one needs multiple green purses or shelves and shelves of beige heels. Yet every week, I help people pare down the dozens of pairs of jeans, the rows of shoes, the piles of jewelry that have become a stranglehold on their lives. So ask yourself, do you already have something at home that is basically just as good? Or indistinguishable from this item? Will you actually really truly use this piece of equipment? Soon, the Instant Pot will go the way of the George Foreman Grill, so most likely the answer is no.

I'll let you in on another secret: when we are window shopping, that is actually the most perfect and beautiful that item is ever going to look. Once you get it home, it will get scuffed, snagged or stained. It will get dusty. It will be just one more thing.

So can you admire it and love it right here without owning it? Can you treat stores like museums? "Oh look, isn't that lovely? What innovative design! Too bad none of this is for sale."

3. Need vs. Want

Do you need these shoes? Or do you simply want them? Not that simply wanting means you can't have. But just saying "I want this" instead of "I need this" is a good exercise to play through. If you say "I need these shoes, because my old golf shoes have a hole in them," well, that's clear, but if you say "I need these shoes, because they go with my Easter dress," well, actually, you *want* to match on Easter. That's a want. How many times have you said "I need another pair of jeans." I'm here to tell people with shelves of jeans that, unless you're a rancher, you don't.

Here's a question that can truly separate out needs and wants: How often are you doing laundry? Once a week? You need nine pairs of underwear. Once every two weeks? You need sixteen. Every other day because you're a family of four? You could probably get away with living out of a suitcase. It's a metric.

4. Trying It On

On almost every job, I encounter equipment or tools or materials for a hobby my client thought was going to be their new raison d'être but that they ultimately did for only a few weeks or months and then abandoned. Yet they have the thousands of dollars' worth of supplies, the state-of-the-art tennis racquet, the six Lululemon yoga ensembles, the cashmere yarn, or the surfboard. When you are learning a new skill, try renting equipment. Yes, it won't be as awesome as what you could buy, but until you know that spinning is really and truly for you, why spend over $100 on shoes or $2,000 on a Peloton bike that is only good for one thing?

Believe me, I understand that trying a new activity brings up insecurity, and the equipment can make you feel more confident. "At least I *look* like I ski." However, I bet you can risk the vulnerability of just showing up! Can you let go of equipment as a buffer to your insecurity? I promise, you will not make any fewer mistakes in Zumba if you're wearing Sweaty Betty.

Additionally, let go of the mindset that if you spend a ton of money, it will force you to follow through on your vision. It won't. The mat and the matching towel and the water bottle and the cute outfit will just make you feel even worse when you figure out that yoga actually aggravates your sciatica.

Please do whatever it is for at least six months before you

buy a single thing. Think of it as an investment and reward once you've demonstrated expertise.

And side note: you can most likely borrow any and all of this equipment from a friend who fell into the same trap.

5. **Shoes vs. Cash**

When I'm drooling over a new purse with a price tag of $250, my teenage friend Kate will say, "Okay, imagine I have the purse in one hand, *but* I have $250 cash in the other. Which do you reach for?"

If I'd rather have the cash, I put the purse back.

Do you remember the episode of *Sex and the City*, "The Old Woman Who Lived in Her Shoes"? Carrie realizes that her hundred pairs of $400 shoes could have been her down payment on her apartment. She had frittered away her financial security one pair of Manolos at a time.

Maybe you'd rather have the cash.

6. **Quality vs. Quantity**

Are you are going to get a lot of wear out of these shoes? Or are they a quick fix? I'm a firm believer that it is so much better to have one $50 T-shirt that looks great for years than ten $5 T-shirts that pill after a wash or two.

In her book *Overdressed: The Shockingly High Cost of Cheap Fashion,* Elizabeth Cline explores the high toll disposable garments are taking on the environment and on the human beings employed in sweatshop conditions to manufacture them. While it may seem harmless to buy a $12 dress on your lunch break, because it's sort of cute and you might wear it, it's actually anything but.

Have you ever found yourself holding an item that kind of fits you okay and thinking, "Oh well, I'll just wear it a time or two, and then if I'm not in love with it, I'll donate it." The fact is thrift shops are overrun. At dClutterfly, we have to drive donations *hours* outside of Los Angeles now to find a place that will take them. Because clothes are so cheap, people don't want secondhand stuff. In fact, you'd be better off bringing the items to a fabric recycling center. H&M, Madewell, and the North Face have started collecting their old clothes at their stores so they don't end up in landfills.

So ask yourself, how long am I going to use this for? Is my home just a weigh station on this item's journey into a landfill? Chances are when you look at it that way, those sequin hot pants will lose their luster.

7. Dopamine Rush

According to research out of UCLA by neuropsychologist

Robert Bilder, PhD, shopping might be getting you high.* Every time we buy something, we get a little dopamine rush, more if the item is on sale. Not long ago, excessive shopping was considered a compulsion; now Bilder and his colleagues argue that it's an addiction. To call something an addiction suggests that "developing a tolerance" for it is possible. Bilder says, "It requires a larger dose to get the same effect. You find yourself needing more and more." That certainly has been the case for clients of mine who have spent tens if not hundreds of thousands of dollars on unworn, unused merchandise.

Recently, after one of my talks, a woman came up to me. Her eyes were darting around. I sensed she was struggling to unburden herself. Finally, when every person was done asking questions and we were alone, she whispered, "I'm a clinical social worker. My job is *extremely* stressful. I go to Marshalls every day after work. There is just something about the *click click click* of the hangers that soothes me. It's my reward." As she said it aloud, she heard herself. I told her that her homework was to find a new reward, one that didn't cost anything or bring more stuff into her home. A few months later, she emailed me that not only had she

---

*   Cecilie S. Andreassen et al., "The Bergen Shopping Addiction Scale: Reliability and Validity of a Brief Screening Test," *Frontiers in Psychology* 6 (September 17, 2015): 1374, doi: 10.3389/fpsyg.2015.01374.

decluttered her home, donating bales of unworn clothes to Dress for Success, but she had adopted a dog, and now her daily reward was coming home to his face and making friends at the dog park.

This comes back to Clutter Block #2, My Stuff Tells Me Who I Am. If you are using shopping to provide social interaction, can you transfer that very real human need to another activity? How about volunteering instead? You can meet friends by walking dogs at a shelter or holding babies in the NICU.

Gratitude can also be hugely helpful and is scientifically proven to replenish willpower. Think of everything you *have* in the moment, and you will want less.

Make an action plan for the next time temptation strikes. Will you text or call a friend or accountability buddy? Maybe you duck into the bathroom to go on a whispered gratitude rampage, where you rapidly list everything you're grateful for, from having working eyes to a functioning body to a roof over your head. Some of my clients will pop in headphones and do a quick meditation in their car. Type up the action plan on your phone or on a card in your wallet, and then you'll know exactly what to do to avoid the transient high of the purchase.

For clients who struggle, I advise them to make it harder to spend money. Take the Amazon and eBay apps off your phone and tablet. Make a vow to only shop in person and pay cash.

This is a classic move taken right from the pages of Debtors Anonymous, but nothing slows your roll like paying cash for everything. Frequently, what we need to do is just slow down, take a breath, and give ourselves the time to think about a few of these eight questions.

So do you want the shoes or the momentary high of the sale and the thrill of the new? If you can't tell, do what dieters do: put them back, go do something else to distract yourself, ideally with something else that will stimulate your endorphins, like exercise. If you still want them, you can come back for them tomorrow.

8. Whittle Down Your Credit

This is a fun one. Do you have debt? If you have your credit card app on your phone, you can choose to make a payment on the spot for the cost of the item you were about to purchase. Now *that* is satisfying.

If, after all those questions, you still choose the shoes, then whoop whoop and wear them in good health. But I promise you that putting every item through this test will decrease what you bring home by between 80 and 90 percent, and whatever you don't bring home, you don't have to care or find a place for!

9

celebrating and inhabiting your new space

LIKE SO MANY WOMEN BEFORE HER, DEBRA HAD COME TO LA in her twenties to pursue a dream of being an actress. Now she was in her fifties, working at an accounting firm, and living in a rent-controlled apartment. Her greatest joy was volunteering for an organization that teaches reading to homeless children.

She called me and confessed that she hadn't had a single person inside her home for twelve years. Her apartment wasn't dirty, but it was crammed full of old books, newspapers, and magazines, and nothing was where it was supposed to be. Tax returns lived on the dining table, bags of bags were in the living room. She just kept saying, "I don't know how it got this way."

Only when we cleared out that top layer did we figure out what was really going on. We discovered, under the magazines and books, her old headshots, audition outfits, workout tapes, and all the accoutrements of a life she hadn't made peace with letting go. She was literally burying the regret.

Once she brought that regret out into the light, she was able to literally and figuratively let it go. What it left was clarity: not just a home she started inviting people over to and an empty guest room for her family to start visiting regularly but the revelation that what really made her happy was the nonprofit. She applied for a full-time position there, left her firm, and started a new chapter of her life, one rich with social and family connection and the professional fulfillment she'd been seeking for thirty years.

It might seem like celebrating your accomplishment doesn't deserve its own chapter, but this is a new era of your life, and as such, it deserves attention. You've done a ton of hard work, physically, mentally, and emotionally. Getting honest with yourself about your relationship to your stuff and your Clutter Blocks is taxing. You might even have had some big cries along the way. Sometimes after a particularly big job, I take a day off to celebrate and restore—and it's not even my house!

Share It!

Take your "after" photos and share them with friends and family or post them on social media. Invite people over, but do it in a way that works with your newfound freedom and ease. If hosting a party has always meant that you have platters and decorations that sit out for months afterward, just invite a couple of friends over for a drink or snacks. If hosting a family holiday was the goal, send out those invitations, maybe with a picture of your newly cleaned space that says, "This is waiting for you!"

Whatever you were blocked from doing in the past—having the team over, hosting poker night, inviting the PTA to make signs and fliers, hosting a clothes or book swap, inviting a guest for the weekend—whatever it was you were waiting for, do it now.

A word about flinging your doors open: I have seen with many clients that they free up the space to host more activities and then realize that, on some level, they don't enjoy it as much as they thought they would. That perhaps they put the physical barriers up because something about entertaining is stressful or triggering for them. That is 100 percent okay. Just because you have cleared your home so you can open your doors doesn't mean you have to. It's okay to just enjoy it by yourself as well or gradually find a way of entertaining that isn't stressful.

It will be a process and a journey to find

how these activities will work for you. Allow yourself that period of experimentation.

Take Stock

This isn't just about a moment of pride; this is about creating an anchor.

During a trying relationship, I gained some weight and was uncomfortable in my body. The process of losing it was hard work. Once I did, I paid close attention to the body I had always previously taken for granted. When I was tempted to comfort myself with food, I had to remind myself how hard I had worked and that nothing would taste as good as healthy felt. That healthy feeling was my anchor feeling.

Your freedom is your anchor feeling, and it will hold you down when you are tempted to buy more than you need or leave what you have lying around. Notice how you feel. These are sentences I am frequently emailed:

"Tracy, somebody called me last minute, and I was able to get out of the house in less than five minutes!"

"My neighbor asked if his daughter could park in my garage while I was away, and I was able to say yes!"

"I now have a choice of shower or bath in any bathroom of my house! They're not storage spots anymore!"

Acknowledge the hard work, acknowledge how good it feels, and let that feeling carry you forward.

Reward Yourself

Almost everyone I work with unearths at least one unused gift card or enough coins to bring to Coinstar. With these buried treasures, treat yourself to an experience or some really nice organizational tools: boxes, folders, labels, or dividers.

In fact, build in regular rewards for yourself. In cognitive behavioral therapy, there is a technique called active self-reinforcement,[*] and the idea behind it is that if we stimulate our pleasure receptors in association with a challenging task, it gets easier and more rewarding, because our brains start making positive associations with the task. So maybe every Sunday afternoon that your house is in order, you take that in, then take yourself for a manicure with extra foot rub. Or you take a bubble bath. Or you give yourself thirty minutes to read a book you've been dying to get to. Soon, your brain will associate putting things away with the positive anticipation of that reward.

---

[*] Frederick H. Kanfer, "The Maintenance of Behavior by Self-Generated Stimuli and Reinforcement," in *The Psychology of Private Events: Perspectives on Covert Response Systems*, eds. Alfred Jacobs and Lewis Sachs (New York: Academic Press, Inc., 1971), 39–57.

Reward Your Home

Now that your house is clutter-free, you may notice that it desperately needs a paint job, or maybe the upholstery under the piles of laundry on the couch is actually worn out. Perhaps your kitchen always gets cluttered because it actually needs to be updated to give you the storage that you need.

Decluttering frequently leads to home improvement, because the home has been revealed. Without all those layers, you can see the house clearly for the first time, and it might need a little love. That's exciting! Who are you now, as opposed to the last time you painted or picked out furniture? How are you using this space now? What do you want it to do for you?

Now that you've conquered your Clutter Blocks, you should be feeling liberated to use your home to reflect your authentic self back to you.

Is it time to turn those newly cleared-out former kids' rooms into a home office and craft space? Do you need a space for grandkids to sleep over? Do you want to start a home-based business and can now annex part of the newly cleaned-out garage?

What if you've let go of a storage facility—or two—in this process? Well, there is your budget for the sprucing up you're planning. You have done the hard work of setting the stage. Now you can truly make this your dream home.

Give "New" Time

It's also okay if you feel strange and catch yourself thinking, "Where did it all go? It's so empty."

If your new home feels uncomfortable or like you're rattling around, that just means that you need a little time for your self-perceived identity to catch up to your new environment. Think of getting in shape, for example. Gaining that strength takes months. You did this extreme makeover in a few hours or weeks. That's a huge change in a short period of time. Your brain needs time to catch up. In the meantime, keep focusing on the positives. "It feels weird to have so much space, but wow, I sure look forward to getting dressed in the morning now that I can find my clothes." One day soon, the uncomfortable feeling will pass. You will feel like you deserve this beautiful, clean home.

PART FOUR

life's big changes

10

downsizing: the purge of a lifetime

WHEN I MET BRUCE, HE'D JUST LOST SHIRLEY, HIS WIFE of more than fifty years, to a long illness. Shirley had not only been a prominent doctor who'd helped pioneer advances in women's health and a strong personality loved by everyone, but she'd made most of the big decisions about their lives. Bruce was left to handle those himself now, and despite her passing so recently, a real estate agent had already gotten her hooks into him. She'd told Bruce that for the house to sell properly, he would need to vacate it within two weeks. This was the house he and Shirley had lived in together for more than four decades. They had raised their children in this house, and it had been the center of their and their friends' social world. It was an epic challenge.

We started on the top floor of the six-thousand-square-foot

property and worked our way down. Every room had to be accounted for. Every closet. Every drawer.

Bruce did surprisingly well. He made quick decisions and easily gave things to friends and family. He kept saying, *I don't need it. I won't use it ever again. Get rid of it.* We donated van load after van load. I was stunned, given the emotional enormity of the task, that he was one of the easiest clients I'd ever worked with, but I kept wondering when the other shoe was going to drop.

Then we arrived at Bruce's scuba equipment. In a room off the garage, Bruce had bins and bins of tanks, wet suits, fins, masks—everything a top diver could want, because once upon a time, he had been one. Now at eighty-three, he was not. When I asked about getting rid of some if not all of it before moving into his new fifteen-hundred-square-foot duplex, he said, "No way. *That* I'm keeping."

His son attempted to help, pointing out that he hadn't been diving in years and, because of health issues, likely wouldn't dive again.

"You don't *know* that." Bruce really dug his heels in. "I'm keeping it. I *know* I will use it again." He told us to pack all the equipment up and move it to the new house.

So we did as told. I knew this wasn't the hill to die on. If he had a vision where the second bedroom wasn't a place for his grandkids to stay but a storage locker for scuba equipment, so be it.

At the new house, the movers got to work unloading the furniture off the truck, and my assistants helped make sure the beds and couches ended up in the right spots. Meanwhile, we sat out on two folding chairs on the lawn to keep out of the way, and we talked. We discussed his wife, his life. We discussed change, its surprising ease in moments, but also the difficulties, the challenges. Finally, the guys began to unload the scuba equipment. It was late in the day, there wasn't much space left, and they wanted to know where they should place it. I watched Bruce's face as giant box after giant box emerged from the last truck onto the sidewalk. He started shaking his head.

I put my arm on his shoulder and asked him what was wrong. Bruce turned to me with tears in his eyes and said, "Diving was my life. When I wasn't working, I was diving. When I *was* working, I was thinking about where I was going to dive next. We planned all our trips around diving. It was who I was. What I did. And now it's not there anymore." Bruce, I realized, was talking to me about Shirley. His whole life.

Sure, the scuba equipment was the vessel, so to speak, and he would miss it, but it was really about Clutter Block #1 and what it represented. Time passing. People dying. Bruce himself growing old. Vanished opportunities. As long as he held onto the diving gear, he was still that young doctor in the Maldives. Except he wasn't anymore. And letting go would give him a chance to be something new. Someone new.

He told the movers to let the boxes be and instructed me to dispose of them the best way I knew how. So I donated them to a scuba school.

After we got Bruce all unpacked and sorted and I told him to think about activities that could be his next interests that weren't exactly scuba diving, but another source of outdoor joy, he mentioned gardening.

Later, he took it up. At a gardening class, he met a lovely woman who was his age, a widow as well, and they hit it off. I see them walking their dogs together sometimes, hand in hand, through his neighborhood.

Downsizing is a very different purge from regular decluttering because it applies to people who may never have had a clutter issue before. What distinguishes downsizing is that there is a forced scalability, meaning you know you're currently living in a four-thousand-square-foot house and will be moving to a one-thousand-square-foot apartment in a retirement community, so you need to move with 75 percent fewer belongings. It stops being about use or fondness and becomes about space—pure and simple.

I love downsizing clients. I love seeing people taking control of their lives and deciding to streamline and set the stage for the next adventure. Typically, my clients are downsizing because they've reached a point in their lives where the place they raised their family is simply too big, expensive, and exhausting to maintain. They are ready to live somewhere that asks less of them and leaves them more time for fun. They're right. Having done it so often, I know how happy they are going to be on the other side. It's like a hip replacement—clients always say to me when it's done, "Why didn't I do this sooner?!" Knowing that is where they get to helps me keep them going through the process, which can be a slog.

In fact, downsizing might be the most stressful of all the challenges my clients face. Everything I've laid out in the preceding chapters goes double for this process. Plan breaks, hydration, snacks, fun music, and, most importantly, support. This is going to be emotional, and that is okay. Expect that Clutter Blocks will come up. You may have been able to hide a Clutter Block from yourself in a large house, but if you're going from fifteen closets to five, you might suddenly be confronting overbuying, fantasy buying, or back IRS statements you've avoided. Nobody needs you to be stoic—you will not be the first person to cry and pack at the same time.

However, I also want to emphasize, because I have seen this repeatedly with my clients, that there is a wonderful opportunity here to move into your next phase lighter. Unburdened by having made all these decisions, you are free to enjoy your next chapter as you have envisioned. I am always delighted when I stop by a client's new home and see that, free from their Clutter Blocks, they've taken up a new hobby or discovered a new passion.

So let that guide and inspire you through what is inevitably going to be a challenging few weeks.

Timetable

Before we get into making decisions about what to take with you, the first step is to make a calendar for yourself, working backward from your hard move date. Because I handle these moves so often for clients, I am including everything you will need to remember here so you can relax and just refer to my checklist. In the resources section there is a copy of this to-do list with space for you to write your own dates and check the boxes as you accomplish your tasks. This will help you stay organized and on track. In general, always give yourself more time than you think you'll need. The items on your calendar in order are:

Set Your Move-In Date

This will be determined by the new facility or by the close of escrow of the new home. Then you'll be able to work backward.

In a perfect world, six months is ideal, but I recently had a client who needed to downsize her father from the large apartment he'd shared with his wife of forty years into a one-bedroom. He had been assured he would be able to rent back the large apartment from the new owners for a few months after closing while his new place was renovated and customized with shower bars and other features. But at the last minute, the coop board forbid him from renting his old place. They essentially evicted him, and he and his daughters had *ten days* to empty a four-bedroom duplex. So anything is possible, but if you give yourself more time, you'll be able to do a little bit every day without feeling overwhelmed. And if you start decluttering long before the question of packing arises, you'll feel more on top of this transition.

If You're Selling Your House, Interview Real Estate Agents

Get a personal recommendation and meet with at least three. Don't necessarily go with the person who tells you the highest listing price. Pick the person you enjoy being with who also has a great track record. Sometimes agents will promise the moon to get the listing. Ask for honesty. Look at the marketing packages for other homes they have sold. Are they savvy on social media? Do they host the open houses themselves, or is it an assistant? It's better if they give you that personal attention. Then early on, have a conversation with the real estate agent you've selected about what needs to be left behind to stage the home or if he or she needs it emptied to get a good price.

Get Referrals and Interview Movers

The sooner you can book a mover, the better you will feel. Also consider hiring the mover to do the packing, especially for things like the kitchen. That is a tremendous amount of physical labor you can save yourself. Again, always get at least three personal referrals from friends or family, and be very, very wary of people who give a flat rate—I have unfortunately encountered more shady movers than I care to remember. Which is why I recommend doing an inventory of everything valuable that gets packed so nothing gets stolen. If this is overwhelming to you, you can also reach out to the National Association of Senior Move Managers. These people are experts and can help coordinate every aspect of your move.

Get the Floor Plan and Exact Measurements
of the New Place

Do *not* pay to move furniture that won't fit in the new place, and do *not* rely on your eyeballs or mind's eye. We all picture spaces as bigger than they are. I recently moved a client into a home that she was excited about because, she insisted, her wingback armchairs were going to look fantastic in front of the fire. Well, once we got them in, they dwarfed the space, prohibiting a couch *or* a coffee table. Have someone get out a tape measure and do some precise math. Also measure every linear foot of closets. That means the length of every hanging bar and the length of every shelf. In general, retirement communities are good with helping with this.

Call Appraisers

I will go into this in depth later, but this is the time to find out exactly what has value and what doesn't. If something is worth selling, and you know you don't want to take it with you, start the sale process by calling auction houses or liquidators. Books are very heavy, expensive to move, and take up a lot of space. Is there a local library, new school, or community college that needs them?

Take a Video of Your Old House

Commemorate how it was before you start dismantling it. Another person told me that when they moved from their lifelong home, they documented it in photos and then had the photos made into a book. Now when they feel nostalgic, they flip it open. Or have a good old-fashioned goodbye party. Invite people who have memories of your home so they can get some closure.

Collect Important Papers

Keep together items like deeds, wills, durable powers of attorney, medical records, military records, diplomas and degrees, birth certificates, and passports. These can be in a file cabinet or safe-deposit box, but let key family members know where they are and what they'll need to access them.

Give Your Family a Deadline

If there are items they've always wanted, share your timeline and tell them to arrange for pickup. This is also the time for adult children to come and get their keepsakes. You no longer need to be the family museum. Having trouble unloading items? Reach out on social media to the younger generation beyond your direct descendants and ask if anyone needs to feather their nest. What about your housekeeper? Do you have a community bulletin board you can post on?

This is also the one time I have ever endorsed getting a storage unit! A client of mine called me in a panic. Her father, who had been a widower for just under a year, had remarried, and his new wife was wholesale throwing out everything that had belonged to her mother. She had just given birth to twins and couldn't make the journey home. I told her to call a moving company and have them come and get everything and put it into storage until she could get back to Iowa and go through it.

Begin the Process of Paring Down Your Possessions

Go room by room, based on how many square feet you have versus how many you are moving to. Refer to the advice given later for specific purging guidelines.

Pack Long-Term Items

Pack whatever you won't need between now and the move, like holiday decorations or seasonal clothes.

Complete Address Changes

Notify:

- O post office
- O credit cards
- O bank accounts
- O investment/retirement accounts
- O Medicare and Social Security
- O voter's registration
- O family and friends
- O driver's license/car registration
- O newspaper/magazine subscriptions
- O social clubs and places of worship
- O lawyer, accountant, insurance agent

Refill All Your Prescriptions

Do this before you move, so you don't have to arrive and immediately find a new pharmacist.

Consider Boarding Pets

Board pets during the move days if you're not going far. I have seen so many moves derailed by stressed pets that hide like Houdini.

Pack a First Box

The one that goes in the car or plane with you filled with whatever you'll want to put your hands on right away to feel at home. What will make you feel good? Your coffee beans and special mug? Your pillow? Pack a week's worth of clothes and toiletries in a suitcase as well.

Arrange for Donations

Coordinate the picking up of donations to be delivered to their respective destinations. Also, remember you might need a trash haul.

The Process of Paring Down

As you stare down the mountain of possessions you have acquired in this life, there are new questions you have to ask yourself that are specific to downsizing. Your life is going to be changing, and those changes should inform your packing decisions. Hopefully this will feel really liberating.

* Are you switching not only size of house but type of house and climate? See if this affects what you keep or discard. Maybe you're moving to a sunshine state and can get rid of the bulk of your winter gear. Can you donate all your coats to a coat drive?

* Perhaps you are moving somewhere where you won't have to drive anymore. You can get rid of all your automotive accessories, all your repair gear.

* Will your new home come with a handyman? If so, maybe all the tools in the garage can be passed along, or if your new place doesn't have a garden, those tools can be donated.

* Can you unload something you always hated doing? If you were always the one hosting holidays, think about passing the torch—and all the endless stuff that goes with it. Do you want to keep doing seasonal décor, or are you happy to give someone else all your ornaments?

- How many beds and bathrooms will your new home have and what sizes are they? Go through your sheets and towels to determine just how much linen you will actually use in your new home.

- Will you need as many suitcases? If you're still holding on to suitcases big enough to accommodate a six-week ocean voyage when the longest you go away for these days is three days, consider donating them to children moving through the foster care system.

- How can this be an opportunity to upgrade or streamline your life? Don't take VHS tapes, DVDs, or CDs. Hire someone to come over and put all your CDs in iTunes. This is a great time to invest in and learn how to use a smart TV or a Sonos or Spotify. Most likely one of the streaming services has all your music already.

- Another way to streamline your life—and eliminate paper clutter—is autopay. My client Lucy had a late husband who had always paid all the bills. At first, dealing with everything was overwhelming, but we got everything put on autopay on one credit card for her, and then she earned enough miles to go on a cruise to Alaska.

- How can you make this move feel awesome for yourself? With the equity you're liberating from your home, this might be the perfect time to think about what you always wanted but never had, like a flat-screen TV or another dream appliance.

* Do you want to style shift? One of my clients had always had a very masculine decor to please her late husband. Now that she was moving to a retirement community by herself, she wanted the home to reflect her taste. Out went all the heavy, dark furniture, and in came white canvas and pink lampshades. This is a great opportunity to curate down to your favorite things.

The New Home Dictates the Terms

Now you want to start thinking very concretely about the new house itself. The first thing you want to do is get the floor plan of where you will be living, along with the exact measurements. Floor plans usually only have approximate square footage. Make sure someone in the space with a tape measure is telling you if your dresser is really going to fit between the window and bookcase. Some retirement communities even offer in-house decorators. Then you can map out what furniture is going to fit there, and that will clarify what you'll want to relinquish.

The next step is to measure all the storage, every linear foot of the closets, existing or planned bookshelves, kitchen cabinets, and any dead storage in the home. Once you know exactly how many linear and cubic feet you'll have to play with, you can work backward from there.

This will help, for example, when you're trying to decide between two platters. If only one is actually going to fit in the new cabinets, that's the one to keep.

If you have to shrink your books down from eighteen linear feet to nine linear feet, you'll know half of them will need to be passed along to libraries or reading programs in your area.

Return to the Five Questions

If a possession is stumping you, this is a good moment to return to the five questions, because the answers are going to be different now:

1. Will you use it on a semiregular basis?
2. Will it make you money?
3. Could you buy it again for a reasonable price or borrow it?
4. Will you have a place to store it?
5. Do you love, love, love it?

Now that you are moving on to this next adventure, the answers might change. You might not need any of the equipment in your home office if you're retiring. You may be happily relinquishing the responsibility of hosting Thanksgiving and delighted to pass along the linens, china, glass, silver, pots, and pans that made hosting possible.

Also, I'm never one to kick the clutter can down the road, but now is not the time to go through photographs, because you will get bogged down. It's too emotional and too time-consuming. Take them all with you and make that one of your first projects in your new home once you're settled.

But it *is* the time to purge your grown kids' fifth-grade artwork and report cards. You can take pictures of special pieces, but you do not need to schlep every piece of their childhoods into your new adventure.

Open a bottle of wine and enjoy going through it all now, either alone or with your spouse. The someday you saved it all for? It's today. Enjoy the walk down memory lane, and then let the bulk of it go.

Across the board, this is the time of the reckoning. Nothing is amorphous anymore. You know exactly who your grandkids are and whether or not they actually want your old Erector set or your piano or anything else you saved for the next generations. Which brings me to…

The Biggest Challenge

What I see my clients run up against every day is wanting their children to take items that they deem valuable but that their children have neither space nor use for. Remember Clutter Block #6, Trapped with Other People's Stuff? Don't do it to anyone else! It's important to accept that your children are living a different kind of life than people once did. They don't entertain on a regular basis, they live in smaller homes, and possessions like china sets are no longer the hallmarks of success they once were. If you insist they take your castoffs, you're putting huge pressure on them.

I say this with love, but your stuff isn't their problem.

I suggest my clients find homes for some of these items outside their immediate family. By putting out a call on Facebook, you might find a connection outside your immediate family who desperately needs all of it, like a cousin or in-law. It will get used and loved, and you'll have the joy of knowing it stayed in the family.

The Question of Worth

Once you have an idea of what you won't be taking with you, you may want to get your possessions appraised should any disputes arise among your family. It's called an appraisal for equitable distribution, and it's vitally important, because the market for antiques has actually collapsed. Right now, midcentury modern furniture is in fashion. The ornate pieces people collected in the '80s? No one wants them.

This can throw people with Clutter Block #6 into a panic. I have done house clearing after house clearing where all of it ends up donated to thrift shops, because the auction houses won't take any of it. The upside is that giving the Victorian sideboard to your daughter-in-law may not put *your* daughter's nose out of joint if she knows it's worthless.

This also goes for "rare" books. *The Antiques Roadshow* on PBS has absolutely warped people's idea of what that old copy of *The Adventures of Tom Sawyer* in the attic is worth.* One of my close friends grew up in a family of rare book dealers, and she says it's painful how often her father has to tell people that their "first edition" isn't actually a first edition but the first printing by that publisher of that title. For example, think of a title by Dickens. There would be the first edition in England—rare and valuable. Then there would be the first U.S. edition—not rare and much less valuable. Then there would be the first editions from other publishers down the line as the rights were passed along and finally it went into the public domain. None of those have any resale value. Remember this

---

* Most likely nothing more than its sentimental value.

about books: as they are relatively inexpensive for readers to buy, publishers have to sell lots of them to make any money. And to sell lots of them, they have to print lots of them. And if there are lots of them, they have less value. Not to mention how many times I have seen a client open a book they thought was valuable only to find it has been eaten away by silverfish. Before you start the bidding, make sure this item is still in pristine condition.

So many times, when I suggest clients can part with something, they say to me, "But it's old." I would love everyone to understand that *old* does not equal *financially valuable*. Old might just mean old. It might mean it is special to your family, but it also does not mean you *have* to keep the sewing machine, the earrings, the butter churn, the saddle, the toiletry kit, or the lamp. Old just isn't a good enough reason to clutter your life.

To get an outside eyeball on your possessions, I strongly recommend hiring an appraiser. See the resources section for a list of ones I recommend. Through their websites, they'll be able to connect you with someone trusted in your area. Auction houses like Sotheby's, Bonhams, and Doyle often offer free appraisals once a month if you take the pieces into them.

Then, appraisal in hand, notify your family that there are pieces they may want, but set a deadline. If they want something, they must come before the moving trucks. Do not move an item someone is telling you they will come for. You are not a storage facility. They come get it now or remember it fondly.

Subsequently, if you have many pieces that no one has claimed, it might be worth considering an estate sale. In my experience, they take a lot of work, and you should start prepping at least three to six months before your move. Most importantly, set your expectations realistically. I say this as someone who has helped hundreds of people set these up. You will hopefully make a couple of thousand dollars. Maybe enough to pay your movers. You will not retire on the proceeds of your estate sale.

One option is also to have the sale after you've left. Blue tape everything going with you, and whatever you leave behind, the estate sale company will sell or remove.

The upside of having the sale after you move is that if you have misjudged and brought something that doesn't fit in your new home, you can take it back and include it in the sale if you've stayed local. You also won't have to witness someone paying a dollar for a Hummel figurine you are convinced is worth hundreds.

You Don't Have to Get It Perfect the First Time

If you're panicking, know you can still purge more on the other end. This is an enormous undertaking. You are going to get decision fatigue. When that sets in, I think it's a little better to err on the side of taking a few too many things rather than getting rid of something you may later wish you'd kept. I often say to clients, sometimes it's better to keep one too many candlesticks than get to the new house and wonder where the crystal pair went.

On the opposite end, frequently when I am helping clients unpack, they open a box, pull out a blanket or a breadbasket, and exclaim, "Why on earth did I keep that?" That is completely fine, totally normal and expected. Do not beat yourself up about it. Sometimes you need to see a possession in a fresh context to realize you no longer want it. Keep some empty boxes on hand as you're unpacking and fill them up with another round of donations.

It Doesn't All Need to be Rational

Remember that brown leather satchel of my grandmother's that lives at the top of my closet? It's still impractical in shape and size. I still will never use it, but it fills me with love and joy whenever I spot it on its shelf. It stays.

You get to keep a few emotional items that may serve no purpose but to fill you with happy memories. That is a purpose and a valuable one.

Advice for Anyone Helping Their Parents Downsize

Above all, be patient. This process is going to be loaded in ways neither of you expect. Your parents (or grandparents) spent a lifetime building a home. Taking that apart, even by choice, is hard. Diplomacy goes a long way. I often say to clients' children, sometimes you just have to take it. The stuff, that is. Take the lamp or the sewing kit or the tea set. Take the item your parent is pressing you to take, and then drop it off at your thrift shop.

The biggest phrase to avoid is: *Just throw it out.*

I have seen that start more fights than I can count! It's just too emotionally loaded, even if you know the item has no present-day value. Instead, say: *Why don't we try and find a good home for this?*

So maybe you take a few boxes of stuff that you're going to "rehouse," and they ultimately end up in the garbage. It's not the end of the world, and this way, you didn't have to confront your parent with the loss.

Be prepared that this process of moving your parents might be a double decluttering for you, because there may be many things you actually want to take, but it means making space in your own home. Don't sacrifice your own home's peace and clarity for your parents' stuff. Make sure you have room before you take anything!

It's also completely okay if you are drawn to an object only to get it home and realize that you actually do not want it. Maybe you have a negative association with it you can't even put into words. Move it right along. No one will ask you whatever happened to Great-Aunt Sally's afghan.

I'll never forget my client Alice. She was turning sixty, retiring from a long career as a nurse, and undergoing cancer treatment. She realized that, should anything not go as the doctors assured her it would, she would be leaving behind a big fat mess. Her entire garage was packed with file cabinets, and each one was stuffed with statistics she had compiled on maternal death rates. She hadn't ever wanted to let any of it go.

What we had to keep reminding her was that all the statistics she had compiled, her life's work, had been digitized. Just because the actual documents themselves were no longer relevant didn't mean her contribution wasn't insanely important. In fact, research papers that had changed the field of obstetrics had been written using her data.

The truth and legacy in memories, the way stuff performed for you when it was needed, can never be taken away, just as letting go of a set of dishes doesn't mean your parents didn't have a wonderful marriage or letting go of a set of scuba gear doesn't mean that you never had a vibrant, athletic life. More often, the meaning or impact outlives the stuff itself.

We cleaned out the entire garage, down to the concrete floor and the wood walls. Alice was starting to feel much better by this point, and this accomplishment had created a new and unexpected inspiration: she could sell the house and move closer to her beloved nieces and nephews. A whole new third chapter was suddenly opening before her!

From the other room, our motivational music switched to "Summer in the City," and we all spontaneously broke out in the twist in the empty garage, me, my crew, and Alice, dancing to celebrate her hard work, dancing to celebrate the newly created space to move and live life on her terms.

11

decluttering after death or divorce

HERE WE ARE, AT THE TWO MOST EMOTIONAL DECLUT-
ters. I call them the nonnegotiables. If life has landed you here, there
is no way around it; this momentous life shift has to be processed
through sorting, packing, and getting rid of stuff. I hope you never
get divorced, but statistically, half of you will. Or you might simply
move in with someone, only to discover you want to move out.
Death—and the cleaning and clearing out that comes with it—is
inevitable. We all go through it at some point in our lives, either
for a parent, a friend, or an in-law. In this chapter, I will let you
benefit from my impartial knowledge and experience to make these
emotionally challenging clearing outs easier.

Transitional Decluttering

One of my specialties is transitional decluttering (or decluttering after someone has passed away), and I feel honored when people ask me to help them. What I've found from the dozens and dozens of these I've done is it isn't like having a new baby, where people jump up to share their experience and advice. I find my clients are frequently completely panicked about where to even start and feel overwhelmingly alone—even though they are probably surrounded by people who have done it at some point. For some reason, people seem to get through it—and then rarely talk about it again.

One way to overcome that is by finding someone in your circles who has walked this walk before you. Call them up or ask them to lunch. Ask for their stories and advice. Ideally, this is someone in your town who might already have done some legwork on where to donate and who to call for help.

I have noticed over the years that people have a weird expectation that the lawyer is going to come tell them what to do. There is no one coming. Make an action plan, who is going to tackle what and when. Start with low-hanging fruit: anything everyone can agree on, like the garage or the pantry. Save items like jewelry and art for last. The more sentimental or valuable, the more potential there is for friction.

If you have the luxury of padding a little time in between the person's passing and the cleaning out of their home, it might make it easier. People will have had time to process their loss and won't be looking to discharge their uncomfortable emotions. Of course, sometimes decisions *have* to be made quickly. One of my clients had parents who lived in a home they could no longer afford with medical bills mounting, but the mother was too sick to move, and the father knew the kind thing was to let her die in the home she loved so much. Within a week of her death, he had listed the house to pay off the bills.

Was it a really hard task to not only pack up their mother's clothes but the entire house? Yes. But his daughters understood the necessity and tried to make the best of it.

There is no right or wrong. If you need to wait a year to have the most perspective, that's great, but don't let indecision and avoidance snowball until tackling this feels insurmountable. I have dozens of clients who simply walked away, leaving their parents' homes intact as a kind of museum to their childhoods. It weighed on them until they finally needed to call me in to help them pack up the homes years later. My advice is to give it time but not too much time.

It is important to recognize that different kinds of loss lead to different kinds of decluttering. In situations of death after a long illness, cleaning might feel great. It could feel good to rid the house of all evidence of sickness—medical equipment, shower chairs, wheelchairs, syringes, medicine bottles—and restore the home to its former glory, when the person you lost was still their best self.

But if you're in shock, you may not want to touch anything. Joan Didion famously left her late husband's shoes by the door for a year so he could put them back on when he returned. If someone has just gone through an unexpected and abrupt change, they may need to have nothing around them change for a good long while.

On the flip side, if you are more than a year out, be mindful that you may be slowing your healing by keeping the home full of painful reminders of what you have lost. It's a delicate balance, so be sure to take all factors into account.

Also, if you are staying in the home after losing your spouse to a protracted illness, I am a big fan of eventually changing things up in the house, even switching bedrooms. Let your brain know that was then, this is now. Caretaking is *hard*, and your nervous system has been through a lot. Give yourself the gift of a fresh start visually.

Strife

In the best-case scenario, you'll have siblings or family who will get in there with you, but I have so rarely seen the best-case scenario. Death can sometimes bring out the worst in people. I say this from years of having been ringside for these assignments, and I think it's because anger is a much more comfortable feeling than grief. One sibling has their hands full and can't come—or won't. I have seen over and over that a family will be moving through the process, getting it done, head down, and a sibling or cousin will suddenly blow through. They are in a fury, upending everything and wreaking havoc, demanding some lamp or telling the people who have been doing the grunt work that they're doing it all wrong. Or they appoint themselves the Lorax of the project and need to speak on behalf of the deceased. My advice is to avoid engaging and allow that person to blow through all their anger so they might be able to get to the grief underneath.

Also, people can get very triggered by the Clutter Blocks of others. For example, the sibling who lives without clutter might accuse the sibling who has the same Clutter Block as their late parent of holding on to too much—and a fight blows up.

Then there are the knock-down, drag-out fights for the items of monetary value. Make no mistake, if you are in a situation where everything needs to be distributed, this can be hugely emotionally loaded. I cannot tell you how many times I have seen siblings steal from each other. But is this figurine or painting truly worth the strife? Getting the painting that hung over the fireplace won't bring your mother back, so is it worth losing the people you have left over it? If you are digging your heels in about an item, ask yourself, is it about control?

While I have seen many fights break out over items that have no monetary value, getting everything appraised up front can't hurt. One method for divvying up possessions several family members want is the family auction. After all the items in contention are appraised, everyone with a claim sits down with equal amounts of Monopoly money that represents their share of the estate. For example, if the thirty items everyone wants are valued at $100,000 total and there are five people with a claim, they each get $20,000 worth of fake money before bidding begins. Then an impartial family member (or neighbor or lawyer) acts as auctioneer, and each person gets to bid on what they want. If you choose to spend your entire $20,000 to outbid your cousin for the Eames rocking chair, that's your choice, but once you're out of your fake money, you can't bid anymore. This way, everyone feels they came away with goods that have an equal amount of value, and if you serve food and drinks, it can even be fun!

Underperformers and Overperformers

In her #1 bestseller *Rising Strong: How the Ability to Reset Transforms the Way We Live, Love, Parent, and Lead*, Brené Brown talks about roles we adopt from childhood, typically based on birth order, called underperformers and overperformers. The overperformers will arrive before dawn and clean until their hands crack and bleed. The underperformers will arrive late and then offer to run errands or pick up snacks. Here is what I have observed and Brené Brown admits about herself: frequently, the overperformers crowd the underperformers out.

When my neat-freak client Alexandra's mother died, she brought me over to be an extra pair of hands because she was afraid her sister wouldn't pitch in. Alexandra started cleaning and cleaning and cleaning, but what I noticed was that her sister was too. Her sister was being incredibly helpful but feeling increasingly overwhelmed by Alexandra's cyclone path through the home. Finally, the two erupted in an enormous argument when Alexandra started throwing out stuff belonging to her sister that their mother had been storing for her.

A year later, Alexandra said to me, "It was my fault. I was so overwhelmed by grief, I needed to stay in motion, and I just couldn't stop. It took us months to start speaking again."

If you are an overperformer, take a breath and step back. Trust if you assign your brother to do the attic that he will, and don't micromanage it. Give him space to step into. If you are an underperformer, acknowledge it and say to your family, "I know I have let you down in the past, but it's important to me to help clean out Dad's things, and I want you to know you can count on me."

Awareness can go a long way to an experience that bonds you instead of breaks you.

Humor Is Essential

It is not disrespectful but the emotional caffeine that will get you through. You may find old porn or sex toys. Best not to judge and be happy the person had a healthy outlet. You may find a fishing rod that has you stop cleaning to reminisce about the disastrous fishing trip in second grade where lightning struck and Dad peed his Dockers. Make space for that in the process. A good belly laugh will keep you going.

By that same token, you may discover something that you wish you hadn't. 1980s porn aside, you may find evidence of an affair or some other dishonesty. This was their life, their messy, complicated human life. Call your therapist and make space to have whatever feelings it brings up for you without derailing you from your goal.

How to Prepare

If none of this applies to you and you are just reading this chapter because you've enjoyed hanging out with me so much you just *had* to keep going, I also have advice for how to put your ducks in a row so that this is as easy as possible on whomever you will eventually leave behind.

I had a client, Honey, whose father had invested wisely with a fortune he made in World War II. He died in the '80s, but his wife lived for another ten years, as their ninety-acre property became more and more valuable, as well as all their other real estate holdings. Honey and her four siblings would frequently try to ask, "What's the plan?" and all their mother would do is quote Louis XIV, "Après moi, le déluge." After me, the flood. Meaning she just couldn't deal with setting up trusts or doing proper estate planning. When she died, she left behind a two-year headache for Honey's husband, the mother's son-in-law and executor. Nothing had been put in order, and it cost millions in taxes.

So for starters, I recommend dispersing your assets while you can still watch others enjoy them. Give your granddaughter the bunny figurine she loves or your son-in-law the Le Creuset you can no longer lift.

I cannot tell you how many times women in their fifties have said to me, "I'm the only one who knows where anything is." Be prepared and plan ahead. Make copies of insurance policies and give them to another person in the family. A great idea is to invite everyone over one evening, open some wine, and give people a tour of your house. Even if they grew up in it! Record the evening and go piece by piece.

"This breakfront was your great-grandmother's."

"This vase I actually got in a yard sale for $3, but I've always thought it was pretty."

Let them know what's what—what's valuable and what's a tchotchke.

Start to purge. If you have clutter, I beg you not to leave it to your kids or grandkids to deal with. Throw out the old papers, the old clothes, the stained linens, the shredded bath mats. The Swedes call it *döstädning* or "death cleaning." While the name doesn't translate so well, I think it's the nice thing to do. It makes an epic task manageable, and they will love you for it.

Divorce

Last fall, I noticed that there was a toothbrush in the cup on my sink that wasn't mine. The man I'd been in a relationship with had left it, and he lived on the other side of the country. As much as we tried, the logistics got to be more than we could overcome, yet I couldn't bring myself to toss it.

Obviously, as a professional declutterer, this was not normal for me, but this toothbrush was tough. So I found myself staring at it and kept asking myself why I was keeping it. Just throw it out! And then I said out loud, "What if he comes back? He'll need his toothbrush."

I realized I was hanging on to the what if. The fantasy of *If he comes back*. Not the reality of *He can't give me the kind of relationship I want*.

We hang on to stuff for all kinds of reasons, and most of the time, they're emotional, not practical. When it comes to a breakup, we are often pushed into a situation in which we have to deal with sorting, packing, keeping, and rejecting a tremendous amount of stuff from a very emotional place. The result can be, well, messy.

Obviously, there are two camps here: those who leave and those who are left. Despite what Gwyneth Paltrow says about "conscious uncoupling," divorce is rarely 100 percent mutual. If the situation is bad, custody of the stuff is typically what you can act out all your feelings through—because the person you actually want to scream at may be long gone.

If You've Been Left

I was helping a client move out of the home she had shared for many years with her soon-to-be ex-husband, and we were tagging the furniture with different colored Post-its for *mine*, *his*, and *donate*. As she kept tagging items *mine*, I kept asking her if she was really going to use it in her new home. To which she replied, "Oh, I'll use it if kills me." She was revenge packing.

When the movers unloaded the truck and brought in the furniture, piece by piece, from her old life into her new life, her face started to fall. She realized she didn't actually *want* to look at any of this stuff anymore, and now it was hers to sort through and donate and recycle. If she had just left it behind, it would have been *his* problem.

Rarely have I found that people want what they take on the other side. It was from a time and place that is no longer.

Later that day, we went to a furniture store to buy her a bed and nightstands. In her state, she told the story of the divorce to the salesman. He nodded his head in commiseration and said, "When I broke up with my ex, I walked out the door with my clothes and toothbrush. I didn't want anything. He could have it all."

She asked, "Really? Do you miss anything?"

"Not a thing. If I wanted to be reminded of him, I never would have left."

If you're trying to heal a broken heart, I highly recommend keeping no more than three items of your ex's clothing and putting them away. Don't sleep with them or cuddle them while you watch TV. After a few months, you'll look at them with more perspective, and they might get turned into rags. Put all the photos in a box, and put the box on a high shelf. You don't have to throw them all out now, but get them off your fridge! Similarly, consider selling any valuable jewelry you were given. Many of my clients use worthy.com. The rest can go to any kid you know for dress-up.

Only keep artwork or decorative objects you bought together if you can display them and not be reminded of the relationship. If it feels like someone is sticking you in the chest with a fork every time you look at it, sell it or loan it to a friend for a few years until it's lost its charge.

And definitely purge the intimate items like towels you shared, sheets you slept on together, or place mats you ate on every night. Give yourself a fresh start, and donate the old ones to an animal shelter. As the wise men from *Queer Eye* say, "You can't start something new if you're sleeping on something old."

If you're staying in the home, shake out the feng shui! You don't want this to metastasize into Clutter Block #1! We've all known people who kept their homes frozen in time after a breakup or divorce as if the person might return. Move the furniture around. Get new throw pillows. Similar to the advice above regarding losing someone to a protracted illness, do something to remind your brain from the moment you walk in the door: *This is now. That was then.* Do something nice for your space to show it some love. If you have some empty shelves where someone else's books used to be, arrange yours to fill the space. Have you had your eye on a vase in a shop down the street? This is the moment.

Tell your space: *I'm still here, and I value you.*

It's the first step to feeling the same way about yourself.

If You're Doing the Leaving

Be as gracious as you can afford to be. If your spouse can no longer have your love, can they have your wok? Or the really good espresso machine your aunt gave you as a wedding present? Only take with you what will work in your new life. Sometimes this can be a cross between downsizing and decluttering (don't take the giant china hutch for your new studio apartment). If this applies to you, read the downsizing chapter too. Because you are moving on to a new life stage freer and lighter, and you want to make sure you set yourself up right.

If There Are Children Involved

What you want and/or need will have to take a back seat to what's best for them, and that is typically about creating as much continuity as possible. This necessity may mean staying put longer than you'd want to and leaving everything looking exactly the same for longer than you can tolerate. However, kids do not need to come home from school to find all the furniture rearranged. That may feel liberating to you, but it's a bridge too far for developing brains that have just been dealt a blow.

In fact, you may want to keep all the wedding photos to show the kids there were good times and they were born into love. You may want to save all the wedding presents for the same reason. At the same time, I encourage parents to slowly, gently allow the living circumstances to catch up to the life circumstances. So after a year, yes, redecorate. Yes, get rid of the golf clubs she never came back for. Allow the space to evolve, but give it time to settle first.

epilogue

I DON'T EVER WANT TO GET CALLED BACK BY A CLIENT BECAUSE they are facing another clutter crisis. I am happy to come for a tune-up or a move, but I don't want someone to fall back into their old habits. I don't have a financial model based on recidivism. I want you to feel like you are about to embark on a new chapter in your life now, one where you have the exact right number of things that work for you, and they all live in a place that helps you thrive.

What I want is to run into you on the street or read in a post that you are liberated, that you lost one hundred pounds of wood, plastic, and china and are taking on life like never before.

Reading this book is the first step in the journey, and it's a *big* step. I am so excited for you. You may have tried to let go of your clutter in the past, or this may be the first time you've tried to conquer your clutter. The tools laid out here will work.

You know the emotional reasons you've been hanging on to your stuff. Better yet, you know how to move through them and not let them keep you stuck. You also have all the tools to do the work, the actual physical work of decluttering and letting go. Really, I'm so excited for you! I know you can do it. I know because I've seen this process work thousands of times with people just like you.

The first step is to dig deep and get honest with yourself. I know how hard that can be. Trust me, I'm not immune to emotional blocks. The other day, I opened a drawer, and it was stuffed full of plastic utensils. They arrive with takeout, and I didn't want to be wasteful or hurt the planet. Instead of recycling them, I was essentially hiding this uncomfortable problem from myself—in my own drawer! I need my drawer!

I had to be completely, brutally honest with myself. I wanted a different outcome, but I wasn't putting the work in. It's the same with clutter. Clutter will creep back in. Holidays will come, and you will get gifts. Sales will happen, and you will buy shoes you don't need. Someone will die, and you'll inherit their old furniture. That doesn't make you wrong or bad. It makes you human, living in the real world. What makes this time around different is that you have the tools to deal with the clutter. You'll know why you're inclined to keep it, and you'll have the freedom to let it go. How exciting is that!

The next thing you know, you'll have agency to say no to clutter coming into your home because you'll have felt what it's like to live without it. You'll know what it's like not to be facing crowded countertops every time you walk in the door. To have extra time and extra headspace. To feel calm and clarity. To feel empowered using your space exactly how you envisioned so it supports your best life. You'll know what it is to be free from your clutter.

I know a life without being beholden to your stuff is yours for the taking. Commit to having the home, the garage, the closet you've always dreamed of. Create the vision and set aside the time to create it. Grab a trash bag, a box of Kleenex, and a corner of clutter and get to work. And when you get stuck, grab this book and figure out what Clutter Block is coming up. I promise, once you identify them, you will be able to work through them. With each cleared countertop, with each empty surface, with every bag of donations, know that I am supporting you, and every bag of donations, along the way.

With peace and gratitude,

tracy

resources

Emotional Resources for Healing Clutter Blocks

* The Sedona Method can help you develop the awareness that emotions, even overwhelming ones, are like pencils—you can hold them or drop them. It is available as an audio course or a book housed at most local libraries. The method is incredibly simple, and you can practice it anywhere, as you're cleaning out a closet or loading the dishwasher.

* Tapping, or EFT, is an incredibly helpful, clinically proven way to alleviate stress around a specific challenge, say letting go of your grandmother's bed, and address the underlying emotions that brings up. There is a book called *The Tapping Solution* by Nick Ortner that is very easy to use, and there are plenty of

videos on YouTube that can teach you the method in a matter of minutes.

◆ A very good book that can help you get to the emotional root of any financial issues is *Money: A Love Story* by Kate Northrup. It looks at money from a holistic, energizing perspective rather than simply a rational, dollars-and-cents one. It has pragmatic advice too, but if you are burying financial information, this can help you figure out why.

Donation Resources

This is a small list of resources to use as you put together items and bags for donations. You can also find this information, along with continually updated resources on my website at tracymccubbin.com.

◆ Before you make any charitable donations of items you've decluttered, please read what the IRS has to say about donating at https://www.irs.gov/pub/irs-pdf/p1771.pdf.

◆ For more information on what tax records to keep, see: https://www.irs.gov/businesses/small-businesses-self-employed/how-long-should-i-keep-records.

Food

- Most local food pantries take donations of almost expired or just expired food. Call your local one to find out their guidelines.

- For more information on food expiration, check out savethefood.com.

Clothing and Shoes

- While donating is a great option to keep clothes out of the landfill and out of your closet, before you box up all your wool sweaters and ship them to the latest tropical hurricane site, make sure you are sending items people actually need. Also, make sure everything you are donating is in good, wearable condition. Donating clothes with holes and stains just means you are making someone else do your dirty work.

- Both Nike and Soles4Souls accept donations of athletic shoes.

- Many people don't realize that emergency rooms accept donations of clothing too. Often when someone has been in an accident, their clothes and shoes have been cut off, so donations of gently used clothing can send someone home from the hospital with dignity.

Luggage

- Kids in the foster care system often show up at their court hearings and temporary homes with all their belongings in a black garbage bag. All foster agencies accept donations of suitcase, duffels, and backpacks. Make sure they are clean, have working zippers, and aren't too heavy.

Bedding and Towels

- If animals touch your heart, donate your old sheets and towels to a local rescue. While you don't want to use a towel that's stained or ripped, the dogs and cats waiting to be adopted won't notice. Here are a couple of national organizations with local chapters.
  - ASPCA: aspca.org
  - Best Friends: bestfriends.org

Toiletries

- Are travel soaps and shampoos from hotels something you grab and never use? Throw them in a shopping bag and drop them off at your local homeless shelter. Personal hygiene products are much needed, and the small size is greatly appreciated. They will also happily accept full-size.

- For homeless women, there is the added challenge that feminine hygiene products are often difficult to come by and expensive. If you buy a brand of pad or tampon that you don't end up liking, consider donating them.

Art Supplies

- Teachers are always in need of supplies for arts and crafts. Your mom's old sewing baskets with hundreds of colors of thread, knitting needles, and that giant collection of *National Geographic* or other appropriate magazines are all items that could make a teacher very happy.

Books and Recent Magazines

- Unfortunately, most of us know someone who is battling cancer. If you have ever sat with someone during their chemo treatments, you know it's a long, tedious, and uncomfortable process. I love to pull together a bag full of beautiful magazines and lighthearted books to drop off for patients and their companions to enjoy.
- Most libraries are struggling with budget cutbacks and often have book sales to raise funds. Consider donating the books you are letting go of to your local branch. But check with them first!

Appraisers and Auction Houses

* The best way to find a reliable appraiser is through one of these three organizations:
  - International Society of Appraisers: isa-appraisers.org
  - American Society of Appraisers: appraisers.org
  - Appraisers Association of America: appraisersassociation.org
* For wedding rings and estate jewelry:
  - Worthy: worthy.com
  - Doyle: doyle.com
* For furniture, art, and home décor:
  - Sotheby's: sothebys.com/en
  - Bonhams: bonhams.com
  - Doyle: doyle.com
  - Everything but the House: ebth.com

Recycling

e-waste

* Most cities have some sort of electronic waste recycling program, so check with your local government website or sanitation company. Don't forget to wipe your data!

- Staples offers free electronics recycling. You can read more here: https://www.staples.com/sbd/cre/marketing/sustainability-center /recycling-services/electronics/
- Some Goodwill stores now recycle old electronics. Check with your local one.
- Target, Apple, and Microsoft all have trade-in programs for old electronics. Offset the cost of your new device by trading in your old device.

Fabric

- H&M accepts all fabric now and gives you a discount on your next purchase.
- Madewell takes recycled jeans you drop off and turns them into insulation.
- Levi's will send you a 20 percent off coupon and a download-able shipping label for your old jeans.
- Eileen Fisher has a program called Renew, where they will take back their clothes and donate them if they are still in good shape. If not, they will recycle the fabric.
- Bras and undies—most clothing donation places won't take them, but this organization does: brarecycling.com.

- More places are adding programs, so keep checking my website at dclutterfly.com for the latest options.

- Lastly, if you want to take your recycling to the next level, TerraCycle accepts and recycles *everything*, for a cost: terracycle .com/en-US.

senior downsizing guide

This timetable is the in-a-perfect-world scenario, so go easy on yourself. You can also find a downloadable version of this checklist at dclutterfly.com/senior-downsizing.

ASAP—FIRST THINGS FIRST

O Determine where you are moving to.

6+ MONTHS

O Set your move-in date.

O Interview real estate agents if you are selling your house.

O Get the floor plan and exact measurements of the new place so you can figure out what of your furniture will fit.

○ Start to interview movers.

○ Get referrals.

○ Research on Yelp.

○ Call appraisers.

After receiving appraisals, decide if it's worth it to have an estate sale or just donate or give away items that aren't going with you.

Take a video of your old house to commemorate how it was before you start dismantling it.

3 MONTHS

○ Book movers and schedule move date.

○ Purchase packing supplies, if you are packing yourself.

○ Start the process of clearing out, room by room.

  ◆ Garage

  ◆ Attic and/or basement

  ◆ Guest room

  ◆ Linen closet

  ◆ Office

  ◆ Living room

  ◆ Dining room

  ◆ Bedroom

  ◆ Kitchen

- Collect and keep together important papers.
- Let your family know of the timeline, and arrange for pickup of items that they may want.
- Start packing the items not needed till after the move.

1 MONTH

Complete address changes. Consider sending out a new home announcement to gather support from loved ones during the big change.

NOTIFY:

O post office

O credit cards

O bank accounts

O investment/retirement accounts

O Medicare and Social Security

O voter's registration

O family and friends

O driver's license/car registration

O newspaper/magazine subscriptions

O social clubs and places of worship

O lawyer, accountant, insurance agent

O If you have pets, consider boarding them and schedule it.

2 WEEKS BEFORE MOVE

O Refill all your prescriptions.

O Cancel utilities, cable, TV, and phone at old home. Schedule installation of same things at your new home.

1 WEEK BEFORE MOVE

O Pack the rest of the house.

O Host an estate sale (if you are having one).

O Arrange for donations.

O Arrange trash pickup.

O Pack a first box. Don't load on the truck but take it with you.

O Arrange a pack day, if moving company is packing.

O Arrange a donation and trash haul.

MOVE DAY

O Perform one final sweep.

O Say goodbye to old home and hello to new home!

index

acknowledgments

To Nicola, without you there would be no book. Thank you for your talent, expertise, and limitless wisdom. For walking me through this journey, holding my hand every step of the way.

To Lucinda, for believing in me and this power of this book. Thank you for championing it from start to finish. Your guidance, wisdom, and vision made it all possible.

To Grace and the Sourcebooks team, for bringing this book into being. Turning the thoughts and ideas that have lived in my head and heart into an actual book. Exactly as I always imagined it. Thank you for your professionalism, hard work, and impeccable eye.

To Cassie and Sabrina, for decluttering all the extra commas and bad grammar. You organized my words into a thing of beauty.

To Jillian, Danielle, and Kelly, for designing and illustrating a book more beautiful than I could have ever dreamed of.

To Ashley and Tracey, for shouting my message from the rooftops and making sure everyone is listening. There are no better cheerleaders than the two of you.

To Carrie, for lending your immense talent to crafting the look and feel of the brand and the business, and for never getting annoyed when I ask for my passwords.

To Hutt, for standing on Larchmont and seeing the potential that I couldn't see. Believing in me every step of the way and showering me with support and a whole lotta love.

To Dave R., for championing me through this journey, especially the most difficult part—the beginning. Your words of encouragement always came at the exact moment I needed them the most.

To Julie, for being in my corner for more than forty years. Thank you for your love, support, and always answering every single text. I am blessed to call you sister, sister.

To Josh, for helping me create a business out of thin air in a Land Rover on a dusty road in Kenya. Without that conversation none of this would be, and for the work we do with OneKidOneWorld. Every day I am grateful for that.

To Lauren F., for being the connector to everyone who made this book happen.

To Dave F., for crossing the t's and dotting the i's, but more importantly, for having my back.

To Katrina at UTA, for seeing what I saw in this book and making all in roads necessary.

To Roger, for helping me finally find my voice.

And to Ian, for being my rock, my biggest fan, and the best brother anyone could ask for. There is no one I would rather go on the wild family journey with than you. Every day I'm glad you didn't fall out of JD's Karmann Ghia.

Finally, to my clients. Thank you for letting me into your homes, closets, and drawers. For trusting me with your stuff and your memories. For helping me find my purpose. This is for all of you.

about the author

Tracy McCubbin always referred to herself as "Obsessive Compulsive Delightful," but who knew she could turn that trait into a booming business? While working for a major television director in Los Angeles, Tracy discovered she had the ability to see through any mess and clearly envision a clutter-free space. Coupled with keen time-management and organizational skills, Tracy soon found more and more people were asking for her help. Before she knew it, dClutterfly was born.

Ten years and thousands of clients later, dClutterfly is one of Los Angeles's premier organizing and decluttering companies. Tracy is a regularly featured expert on Hallmark's *Home & Family*, has a column on MindBodyGreen, and hosts regular decluttering segments on Fox 5 and ABC Eyewitness News, the KTLA Morning Show, KCAL9, and Good Day Sacramento. She and her company have also been featured in *Real Simple*, *Woman's Day*, and *ShopSmart*.

When not decluttering, she is the proud co-executive director of OneKidOneWorld, a nonprofit building strong educational foundations for children in impoverished communities throughout Kenya and Central America.

She lives in Los Angeles and knows where her keys are.